$\mathscr{S}$ILK RIBBON
EMBROIDERY

SILK RIBBON EMBROIDERY

Sheena Cable

NEW HOLLAND

First published in 1996 by
New Holland (Publishers) Ltd
London • Cape Town • Sydney • Singapore

24 Nutford Place
London W1H 6DQ
UK

P.O. Box 1144
Cape Town 8000
South Africa

3/2 Aquatic Drive
Frenchs Forest, NSW 2086
Australia

Created and produced by
Rosemary Wilkinson Publishing
4 Lonsdale Square
London N1 1EN

ISBN 1 85368 766 9

Art editor: Sara Kidd
Photographer: Caroline Arber
Copy Editor: Rosemary Wilkinson
Illustrator: Carol Hill
Template artwork: Eileen Batterberry

Reproduction by Hirt and Carter (Pty) Ltd
Printed and bound in Singapore by Tien Wah Press (Pte) Ltd

CONTENTS

Introduction   6

First Steps   8

Stitch Library   14

The Projects:

Laurel Wreath Cushion   30

Barrel Cushion   34

Lacy Bed Cushion   37

Heart-shaped Bed Pillow   40

Thai Silk Cushion   44

Pillow Case & Sheet   50

Pelmet & Tiebacks   53

Tablecloth & Napkins   58

Calico Hat   61

Sunflower Hat Band   64

Chinese Linen Blouse   67

Evening Wrap   70

Evening Waistcoat   73

Gift Box   77

Padded Picture Frame   83

Christening Gown   87

Four Greetings Cards   91

Picture Bow   98

Folk Quilt Sampler   102

Rose Gift Box   107

Spiral Topiary Tree   110

Round Topiary Tree   114

Flower Garden Sampler   118

Index   127

Acknowledgements and Suppliers   128

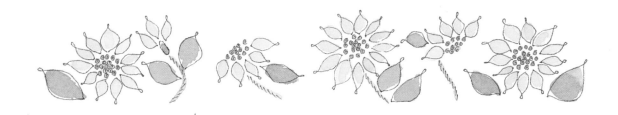

*I*NTRODUCTION

When I was asked to write this book there were certain things I immediately thought about, that were very important to me. Firstly, I wanted to make the instructions to my projects as easy to follow as possible to make them accessible to everyone. So, as well as the step-by-step details for stitching and making up the pieces, I have added 'notes and tips' in various places to give extra pointers to success.

Secondly, I wanted the book to have something for everyone. Therefore the projects cover different degrees of ability, ranging from the absolute beginner, such as the 'Barrel Cushion' on page 34, to those that pose a bit of a challenge, such as the 'Round Topiary Tree' on page 114. As silk ribbon embroidery has only just made a revival in some countries in the last two years, I have tried to make most of the projects easy enough for people with little or no previous experience. You will find it most helpful, if, before you start, you take the time to read the opening chapter on both the materials and the methods. However tempting it may be to get going straightaway on a project that has caught your eye, a little preparation is really worth the effort. The following chapter contains illustrated instructions for making all the stitches contained in the projects.

As you will see from flicking through the pages of my book, I have covered a varied range of projects from table linen to simple greetings cards, hat bands to quilted samplers. I hope that within these pages you will find not only something that attracts your eye but also some-thing that may become useful to you. Perhaps that unusual, and very personal Christening or wedding gift that you have searched the shops for is here in my book: an heirloom item that, if cared for, can be handed down for a number of generations.

Silk ribbon embroidery, or Rococo embroidery as it was also known, started in France around 1750. It was used extensively in the French courts on the gowns worn at that time. Very shortly afterwards it was brought to England for the very same purpose.

From the U.K. silk ribbon embroidery was taken out to America, Australia and New Zealand. The Americans started to cultivate mulberry trees in order to produce their own silk, however, the Orient was able to produce a much cheaper and more plentiful supply of silk, so now most of our ribbons come from the Far East.

In the late 1800s the art made one of its many revivals. At this time, beautiful variegated ribbons were being produced in France and used throughout the U.K. and the U.S.A.

Silk ribbon embroidery has gone in and out of fashion since the 1800s. The Victoria and Albert Museum in London has some fine examples both on display and in its reference section. One very pretty example is an English bag in black velvet, dated 1840. It is embroidered in silk ribbon and crepe gauze. The work is very delicate but has certainly survived through time.

Throughout the late 1800s, articles in ladies' magazines gave ideas for the use of ribbon embroidery; many

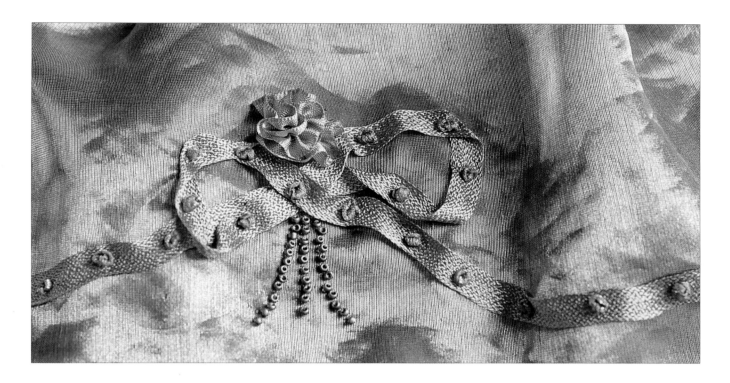

suggested using it with lace and satin ribbons on items such as parasols, evening bags and ball gowns.

The Victorians enjoyed a huge revival of the art. They used it with many other materials, such as beads, lace and buttons and they worked it onto many different pieces, including fire screens, gloves, hats, evening bags and garments. Photography became very popular so, in order to display their treasured family photos, the Victorian ladies worked elaborate embroidery with silk ribbons, lace and beads onto lush fabric to be made into picture frames.

The current revival of silk ribbon embroidery started around 1987 in Australia and has swept through both Australia and America. It is now becoming very popular in the U.K. The wide selection of silk ribbons available in a fabulous palette of colours makes the art accessible to all. You can start off with just a small piece of fabric and a few ribbons. The style of contemporary work varies from period style to abstract and, as you will see from this book, it can be used on many things from clothing to bedding and table linen. I sincerely hope the art of silk ribbon embroidery will not die out this time. I myself intend to do everything I can to help it remain with us.

Sheena Cable.

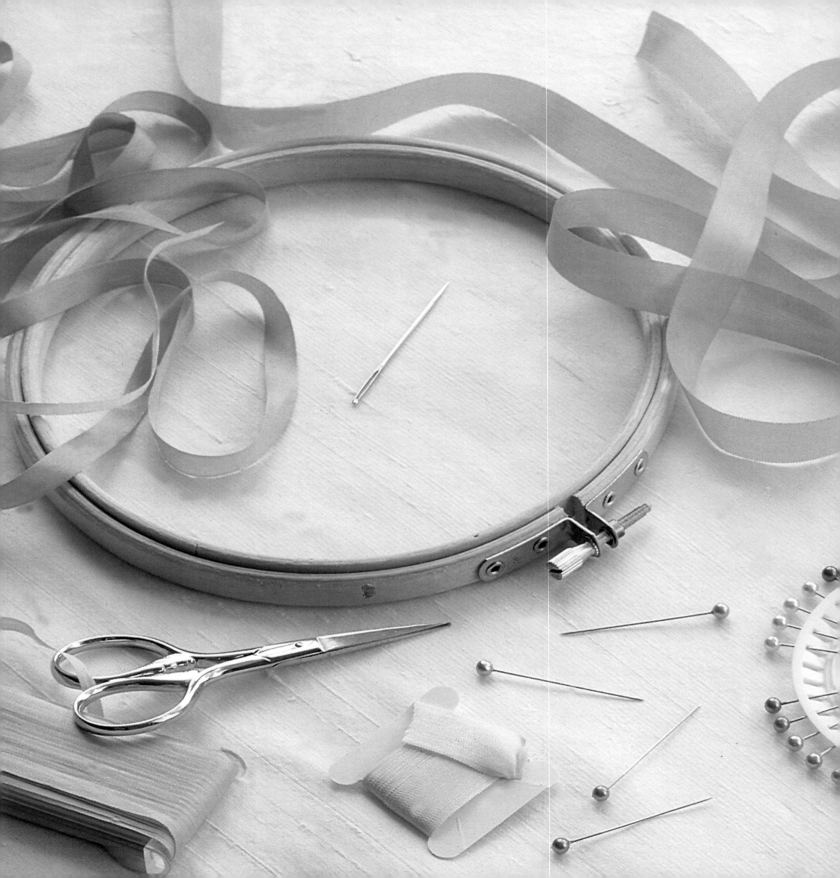

FIRST STEPS

Needles

You will need chenille needles for embroidering with silk ribbon, as they have a large eye. My favourite needle is a chenille no. 18. There are other sizes of chenille needles but the thickness of the no. 18 needle works all the stitches in all the widths of ribbon beautifully. For the embroidery floss work you can use any embroidery needle you feel most comfortable with. A crewel needle which has a sharp point and medium length is the most popular choice.

Other work items

There are a few other essential items. To start with you do need to work with your fabric in a frame or hoop of some description to keep the fabric taut, so that you can judge the correct tension for the stitches. For the projects in the book I have used embroidery hoops of varying sizes, from a 13 to a 30cm (5 to 12 in). The size of the project really determines the size of the hoop. My favourite size is a 20cm (8in) as it accommodates most of the stitching motifs and on projects in this book where the hoop size is not specified, it is more

than likely that I have used a 20cm (8in) hoop.

A plastic clip frame can be used instead of a hoop. It works well as it doesn't mark the fabric and is nice and chunky to hold in your hand. On a couple of occasions for larger items, I have used a tapestry frame. The choice of hoop or frame really comes down to personal preference, choose the thing you are most comfortable working with.

Pins are always required as well as a sharp dressmaker's marking pencil in a pale colour or tailor's chalk. A tape measure with both imperial and metric measures is an essential.

And lastly you will need a sharp pair of embroidery scissors.

Ribbons

Throughout most of this book, with the odd exception (where noted), I have used YLI pure silk ribbon. Pure silk ribbon has a feel all of its own. It lends itself beautifully to the production of flower petals and foliage: as in nature, no two petals are ever the same. Silk ribbon comes in various widths: 2mm; 4mm; 7mm; 13mm and 32 mm: 4mm tends to be the most popular and widely used. The thinner ribbons are used for smaller details and more delicate work.

There are now a number of man-made ribbons on the market and I have stitched with some of these ribbons in the book. I particularly like working with the variegated ribbons, as these were the type (in silk) originally used to embroider French court dress in the eighteenth century. Man-made ribbons definitely have a place in the ribbon embroidery world. I would recommend, however, that you do only use those that have been specifically manufactured for embroidery work to avoid any disappointment when washing your finished work.

I also use double-edged satin ribbon to make roses and wire-edged ribbon for bows and sometimes for roses on display work that I know will never be washed.

Quantities

Companies are now selling silk ribbon in handy pre-wound bobbin packs, usually measuring between 2 and 5 metres (2 to 5 yards). To avoid disappointment, I would always buy half a metre (½ yard) more than the project suggests, as not everyone works with the same tension or to the same scale.

Other threads

Six-strand embroidery floss is used to add detail to the silk ribbon work and to provide the basis for some of the silk ribbon stitches, such as the spider's web rose. Only small amounts are needed, especially as you usually only work with two strands at a time but it is useful to have a range of colours to match the ribbons. Its chief use is to add stalks and stems to floral designs, so a good selection of shades of green is particularly useful.

Coton perlé is a thicker thread than the embroidery floss but is used in the same way. Gold thread is also used to add highlights to a silk ribbon design.

Beads

Beads are a natural embellishment for silk ribbon embroidery. I have used small pearl and glass beads in this book but you could also use bugle beads.

Fabrics

I would thoroughly recommend that the learner silk ribbon embroiderer goes out and buys 50cm (½yd) of calico fabric. I love calico, it has quite an open weave and stretches well on a frame, it is the perfect fabric with which to start.

Many other fabrics lend themselves to silk ribbon work: damasks, linens, cottons, moiré taffeta, velvet and, of course, all the silks. I have tried to use a large variety of fabrics in my book to show how well the embroidery adapts to each fabric. Sheers and stretchy fabrics are not suitable for this kind of embroidery.

Laundering

Silk ribbon embroidery can be washed successfully. If you plan to work with strong coloured ribbons on a light fabric, it is advisable to pre-wash the ribbons. Just a short soak in cold, salted water will be enough to wash out any surplus dye and set the remaining colour. Alternatively you can wash the ribbons in a mild detergent.

I have found it is worth checking if the fabric you are working with will shrink before you work your embroidery. Either check at the shop of purchase or measure an 8cm (3in) square and pre-wash it in detergent.

Once you have finished a project and need to wash it, the best way I have found is to place the item in either an old pillowcase or a stocking holder and wash in the machine on a low temperature (woollen wash) using a mild detergent. Do not spin or tumble dry the item, simply hang it out to dry. If the embroidery looks a little flat when dry, just spray it with a little water and it will pop back into shape. It only remains then for you to iron the item avoiding the embroidery.

Stitch diagrams and templates

Stitch diagrams are given for most of the projects in the book. Where a full size diagram is given, it can be transferred directly to the fabric. To do this, I suggest that you make a copy on tracing paper, then transfer it to the fabric using a dressmaker's marking pencil. Alternatively, you could just mark it out free-hand if you prefer. An exact copy is not important. Where templates are given, trace the outline onto thin card or template plastic and cut out, then draw round the template onto the fabric using tailor's chalk or marking pencil.

Starting off

When working with silk ribbons you must always cut them on the cross (diagonally) to avoid fraying. Work with short lengths of ribbon: no longer than 25cm (10in) for the narrow (2 and 4mm) ribbons and even shorter lengths for the wider ribbons, otherwise the ribbon will fatigue and ladder.

I recommend you secure the thread onto the needle. To do this, first thread the ribbon through the eye of the needle leaving a tail of about 1cm (⅜in), then stab the point of the needle through the ribbon as shown in the photograph. Now take hold of the long tail of ribbon and gently pull the ribbon down until it locks onto the eye of the needle. All that remains then is to tie a knot (just an ordinary reef knot) at the end of the ribbon and you are now ready to begin.

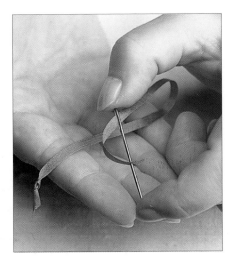

Tension

When completing a stitch, allow the ribbon to lie relaxed on the surface of the background fabric, rather than pulling it taut. In this way the ribbon will form its own soft shapes.

Finishing off

When you have finished a length of ribbon, bring it to the back of your work and trim off the end diagonally. Now thread a crewel needle with sewing thread and attach to the loose piece of ribbon. Do not sew it down to the fabric, as this may be seen from the front of your work. Just work a few stitches to secure the loose end to a previously worked stretch of ribbon, then cut the thread. It is better that you finish off each area of work rather than carrying the ribbon across the back of the fabric to another area, since it is so easy to catch the ribbon and spoil the work that you have already completed.

Pinning ribbon

When working a bow or a curved line of ribbon, I always pin the ribbon very firmly in position first. It is important that the pins are close

together to prevent the ribbon from being disturbed. It is impossible to reposition it once it has been stitched down.

Stitching beads

You will need to use a beading needle which has a long, very thin shaft, since the holes in seed pearls and small glass beads are very small indeed. When stitching a number of beads to my work I tend to use a sort of running stitch: I do not finish off after each bead but bring the needle up through the fabric, through the bead, down through the fabric, then back up again and through the next bead and so on until the correct number of beads have been attached.

Making a tassel

It can get very technical when giving details on how to make a tassel, describing warp and weft and such like, not to mention using a jig. For the projects in my book, I have worked very simple tassels using the simplest of materials: embroidery floss, a piece of sturdy card and a pair of scissors.

Firstly, decide on the length of the tassel, cut a piece of card to that depth and about 5cm (2½in) wide. Take the embroidery floss and wrap it round the card lengthwise approximately 20 to 30 times; the more times you wrap, the fuller the tassel will be.

Cut the thread, then cut a small length of the same floss and thread onto a needle. Pass the needle under the floss on the card at the top edge and take half the thread through. Remove the needle and tie the thread very tightly, to gather up the top of the tassel.

Cut the floss from the card along the bottom edge, then take another length of floss and tie it round the tassel about 1cm (⅜in) from the top, wrapping the thread three or four times before tying off. Trim the bottom of the tassel to neaten it.

STITCH LIBRARY

This section contains all the silk ribbon embroidery stitches used in the projects throughout the book. The photographs show the stages in making the stitches as well as the finished stitch with its correct tension. I've included my hands in some of the photographs where it's important to see how to hold the ribbon or needle.

It's worth practising these stitches on scraps of material or you could make up your own stitch sampler in the same way as the Flower Garden Sampler on page 118. Details are often added with embroidery floss. Stem stitch is the most common but back stitch and fly stitch are also often used. These stitches are given at the end of the library. There are also instructions for a rose using satin ribbon. Please note that I have shortened the length of the ribbon when making some of the stitches just so that it makes a clearer photograph. All the stitches should be worked as normal, i.e. starting with a 25cm (10in) length as described on page 12.

Straight Stitch ▶

This is a universal stitch used for petals, in basket weave (as in the Topiary Tree projects on pages 110 and 114) and in abstract or geometric designs.

1 Bring the needle up through the fabric. Hold the ribbon straight against the fabric away from the direction in which you wish to work the stitch, by keeping it fairly taut with a second needle held in your other hand.
2 Take the needle back down into the fabric at the point which is correct for your stitch length, still holding the second needle under the ribbon to prevent the ribbon from twisting. Pull the ribbon through until the stitch is fairly taut but not so tight as to pucker the fabric.
3 The finished stitch should lie perfectly flat to the fabric. Sometimes, however, you actually want to work a twisted straight stitch. In this case, add the twist to the ribbon before holding it taut with the second needle.

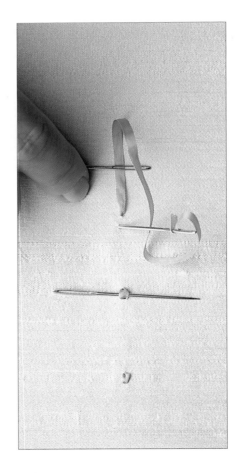

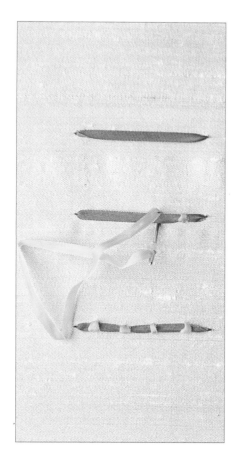

the ribbon over the existing ribbon and back down under the ribbon. Make the stitch quite firm.

3 Carry on along the length of the ribbon, spacing the couching out as evenly as possible. Note that in the photograph I have left the couching quite loose so it is possible to see the work clearly. The firmer the top stitch the more gathered the stitch will become.

Ribbon Stitch ▶

I think this is possibly the most popular and most widely used stitch of all: for petals, leaves and abstract work.

1 Bring the needle up through the fabric at the point which will be the base of the leaf or petal. Lay the ribbon onto the fabric in the direction in which you wish the stitch to go. Holding the ribbon down, pierce the ribbon in the centre at the length you wish the stitch to be. Take the needle down through the ribbon and the fabric.
2 Pull the ribbon through until you get a roll, then very carefully pull through slowly until you have a leaf shape. If you pull the ribbon

through too far you will end up with a thin line of ribbon which is unfortunately irretrievable. The key to this stitch is to work it very slowly.
3 To make a puffed ribbon stitch, instead of laying the ribbon flat, push it back towards the point at which you brought the needle out, then take the needle down through the ribbon as before.

Couched Straight Stitch ▲

This stitch can be worked as a border to edge a piece of embroidery or to work an initial.

1 Work one straight stitch (see page 16) to the length required either vertically or horizontally.
2 With either the same colour ribbon or a contrasting colour come up underneath the ribbon. Take

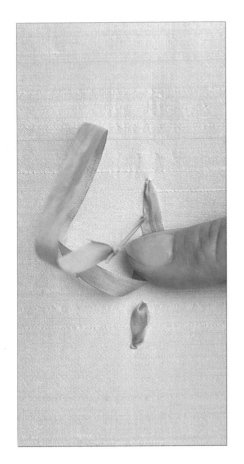

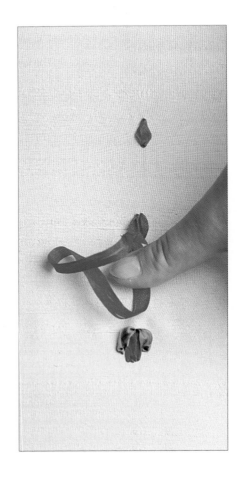

a side ribbon stitch or the slightly fatter shape of a ribbon stitch.

1 This stitch is worked exactly the same as the ribbon stitch except you pierce the ribbon at the left or right-hand side before taking the needle back down into the fabric.
2 The working of this stitch creates an interesting twist or curve to the stitch and is great for leaves and petals. You can choose to curve the stitch to the right or to the left, depending which side of the ribbon you pierce.

Back-to-back Ribbon Stitch ▶

This stitch is wonderful for working rosebuds, and, as the photograph shows, with a smaller ribbon stitch worked in green on either side it looks very realistic.

1 Work one ribbon stitch in the normal manner (see page 17).
2 Work a second ribbon stitch next to the first stitch, starting at the bottom as near to the first stitch as possible. I tend to work both of these using side ribbon stitch so that the top points of the stitch sit back-to-back more

Side Ribbon Stitch ▲

This stitch is used instead of the ribbon stitch on page 17 when you wish to give a particular slant to a stitch. When to use ribbon stitch and when side ribbon stitch on a flower head is a matter of personal choice. Once you have worked a few petals in ribbon stitch, you will be able to judge whether the space left is better suited to the curve of

closely. Take your time with this stitch, it is very easy to pierce the first stitch while working the second.

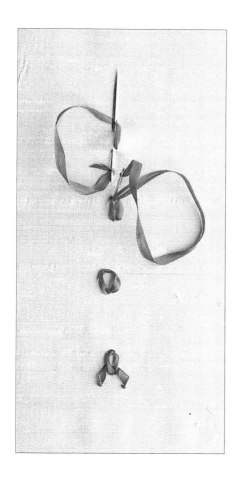

the stitch, keeping the loop of the ribbon underneath the point of the needle.

2 Pull the ribbon through the fabric until the loop is the required size. Do not pull it too tight. To anchor the loop take the needle back down into the fabric just the other side of the loop.

3 To turn this into a simple iris, bring the needle up again slightly below and to the right of the bottom of the stitch. Turn the needle round and go under the chain (needle eye first), then pull the ribbon through fairly loosely. Take the needle back down into the fabric at the same distance from the bottom of the lazy daisy stitch at the left-hand side. Chain stitch is formed when the lazy daisy stitches are worked in an unbroken line.

Lazy Daisy Stitch/Chain Stitch ▲
This stitch is used for flowers, particularly irises, for leaves, petals and abstract work.

1 Bring your needle up through the fabric. Pull the ribbon through and loop it round. Take the needle back down through the fabric next to where the ribbon emerges, then up again at the desired length of

Blocked Lazy Daisy Stitch ▶
As its name implies, this is a solid version of the open lazy daisy stitch described above.

1 Work one lazy daisy stitch as previously shown. Bring the needle up at the bottom of the stitch and

make a loose single straight stitch through the middle.

2 The centre stitch can be worked in the same colour as the lazy daisy or in a contrasting shade.

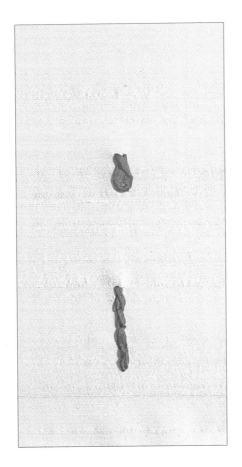

require the stitch to be, with the ribbon looped round the top of the needle. At this point, before you pull the needle through, take hold of the loop and twist it to form a figure of eight over the needle. Pull the ribbon through, then take the needle back down above the third stitch to secure.

2 Bring the needle up just above the first stitch and repeat until you reach the required length of chain.

Merrilyn Bow ▶
This bow was developed by Merrilyn Heazlewood, a top silk ribbon designer and teacher. It is especially suitable on projects that are likely to be laundered regularly.

Twisted Chain Stitch ▲
A useful linear stitch which can be worked in a straight line or curved.

1 Bring the needle up through the fabric, loop the ribbon round from left to right, then take the needle back down next to the point at which you came up. Come up again through the fabric above the first two points at the length you

1 Using any width of ribbon and working from the centre of the bow out, work one large lazy daisy stitch (see page 19) horizontally to the left of the centre. The size of the lazy daisy stitch is determined by the size of the bow you require.

2 Work a second lazy daisy stitch horizontally to the right of the centre. Bring the needle back out at the centre again and work one long stitch downwards to form one of

the bow tails.

3 Take the needle back to the centre, come up through the fabric and work a second tail. Make the second tail a different length from the first and, if you like (and I think it looks even better), add a twist to the tails. Go back up to the centre again and work a small diagonal straight stitch over the centre of the bow.

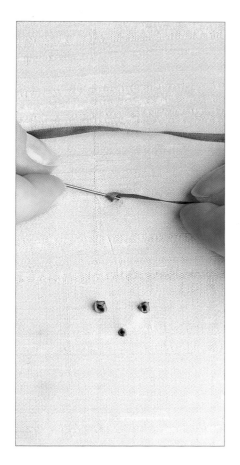

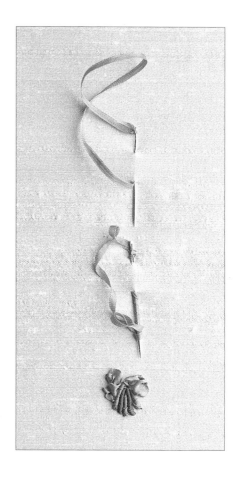

2 Take the needle back down into the fabric as near as you can to where you came up.

You can regulate the tension and ultimately the size of the knot by holding the ribbon in your other hand and keeping it either fairly taut or loose round the needle.

Bullion Stitch ▶

This stitch can be used to form flowers and for abstract designs. It is a good stitch for working on garments or bedding, where laundering will be frequent, as it is firmly secured to the fabric.

1 Bring your needle up through the fabric, noting that this point will be the top of your bullion stitch. Take the needle back down into the fabric at the required length of the stitch, then back up again as near to the point where you first came up as possible without going into the same hole. Do not pull the needle right through the fabric, only about half way.

2 Take the ribbon and wrap it round the needle as many times as necessary so that it will cover the length of the stitch required.

French Knot ▲

This is used for the centres of flowers and is excellent for greenery in clusters. It is also used for securing scrolls of ribbon to the background fabric.

1 Bring the needle up through the fabric. Twist the ribbon once around the point of the needle (twice for a bigger knot).

Gently pull the needle through the fabric and take it back down next to the bottom stitch. Pull the ribbon through very carefully until the bullion is lying close to the fabric.

3 Beautiful roses can be worked using bullions in toning colours surrounded at the base with petals in 7mm puffed ribbon stitch, as shown in the photograph.

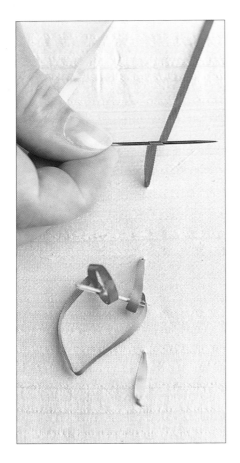

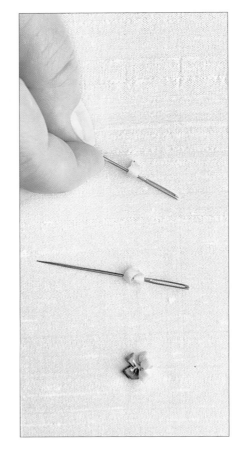

(see page 16), hold the ribbon away from the direction in which you want to go, using a second needle (this guides the ribbon and stops it twisting as you stitch).
2 Before you take the needle back down into the fabric, wrap the ribbon around the needle (in the same way as for a French knot).
3 Take the needle down into the fabric, controlling the tension of the ribbon with your left hand (right, if you are left-handed).

Loop Stitch ▶

Worked in 4mm variegated ribbon, this makes an attractive flower.

1 Bring the needle up through the fabric at the centre of the flower or at the point where you wish the finished loop to be. Make a loop over a second needle or a pencil, depending on the size you wish the finished loop to be. Take the needle back down into the fabric next to the start of the stitch, making the loop the desired size.
2 Come up through the fabric again close to the first stitch and make a second loop, passing the loop over the same needle or pencil

Pistil Stitch ▲

This stitch, as its name suggests, is wonderful for working the pistils on flower heads but it can also be used in any abstract design. Its length is determined by the size of the flower being worked - the pistil must be in scale with the petals.

1 Bring the needle up through the fabric and, as in the straight stitch

to ensure that it is the same length as the first. Work round in a circle to make a flower, always keeping two loops on the needle or pencil to keep an even size throughout.
3 To finish off you could either work two or three French knots in the centre or work a pistil stitch (see left) in embroidery floss into the centre of each loop, as shown in the photograph.

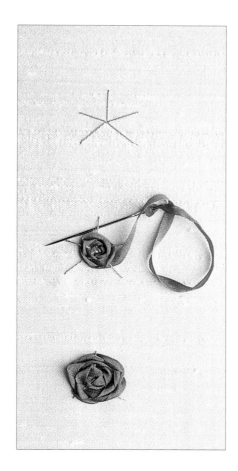

colour to the ribbon.

2 Now using ribbon and starting at any point, come up through the fabric close to the web centre. Take the needle under the first stitch of the web and over the next. Continue in this way, working alternately under and over the embroidery floss stitches. Keep the ribbon tension fairly loose and give it a slight twist with each stitch.

3 Continue working round and round until you reach the outside of the web. Take the ribbon back down through the fabric. This rose can look very attractive if worked well and in two different ribbons.

Coral Stitch ▶

A very pretty stitch used to form flower heads when worked in a circle as here or it can be stitched in a line. Practice makes perfect with this one. I have used variegated ribbon which adds to its charm.

1 Start with three French knots (see page 21) to form the centre.

2 Bring the needle up on the right-hand side next to the French knots. Take the needle down and up again pointing out from the centre and

Spider's Web Rose ▲

This is a good stitch to work on garments or household linen as it is firmly fixed to the fabric with no loops or loose ribbons. These roses look good either on their own or in a group with other flowers.

1 Work a spider's web (five stitches) using two strands of embroidery floss in a matching

wrap the ribbon over the top of the needle then under the point of the needle. Pull the needle fully through the fabric.

3 Continue round the French knots for a complete round, then repeat to make a second round. Keep the stitches close together. The tension determines how loopy the stitch is and you should try to keep the loops as even as possible.

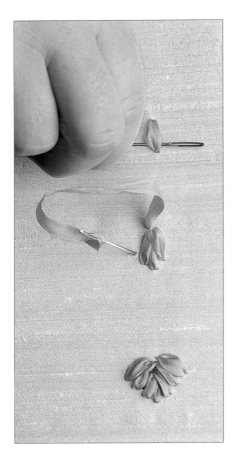

2 For the second stitch, bring the needle up at the bottom of the first stitch and go down into the fabric to the left and slightly below the top of the first stitch. Start the third stitch at the bottom of the second stitch and bring it out to the right of the first stitch, take the needle down to the right and slightly below the top of the centre stitch. Continue like this working left, right, left, right, until the flower head is the size you require.

3 To finish off, as an option, as shown in the photograph, I have worked the odd single stitch in a different colour in between the main stitches. I have just tucked them behind the main stitches using the eye of a needle, to form a contrast and a little more interest.

Fishbone Stitch ▲

Used to work roses, this looks good stitched in toning ribbons.

1 You can work this in a line but for the purpose of demonstration I have worked a flower head. Work one straight stitch to form the centre of the flower. The length of the stitch determines the size of the flower.

Whipped Running Stitch ▶

This is a great stitch for defining shapes, forming words and neatening the edges of basketwork.

1 Work a row of running stitches in any shape to suit your pattern or design.

2 With a second ribbon (either the same or contrasting colour), come up through the fabric at the end of the running stitches, then pass the needle underneath the first stitch from left to right (or vice versa if left-handed).

3 Work all along the running stitches in the same way trying to keep the stitches smooth and the tension as even as possible. You could double wrap each stitch for a moreraised, rope effect, if liked.

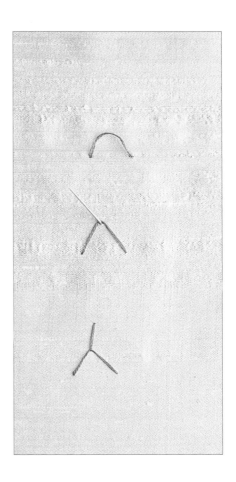

ribbon on top of the 7mm with one edge aligned. Knot the end of the ribbons. Knot a length of sewing thread and sew through the ribbons at the knot end. Work a small running stitch through both ribbons along the edge.

2 Un-thread, then re-thread ribbons and sewing thread into a chenille needle. Come up through the fabric at the desired point. Un-thread the chenille needle and with a new length of thread and a small needle, come up through the fabric next to the ribbon. Gather a little of the ribbon at the fabric end and stitch down. Gather a little more and stitch down. Work round and round, gathering and stitching down, making the stitches underneath the previous round to get a tight ruffle.

Pre-gathered Rose ▲

A pretty, full-blown rose, which can be worked with just one length of 7mm wide ribbon or with a second length of 4mm ribbon in a contrasting shade.

1 Cut a piece of ribbon 28cm (11in) long or one length of 7mm and one of 4mm in another colour. If using two ribbons, lay the 4mm

3 When you are left with just 4cm (1½in) of ribbon, re-thread the chenille needle and take the ribbon back down into the fabric just after the last stitch. Sew down at the back and cut off the tails.

Fly Stitch in Embroidery Floss ▶

A useful stitch for adding calyxes to flower heads.

1 This stitch is worked from top to bottom. Bring the needle up through the fabric. Take it back down to the right of the first stitch on the same line and, in the same movement, bring it up again through the fabric below but midway between the two stitches.

2 Pull the thread through and take the needle down into the fabric below the central stitch.

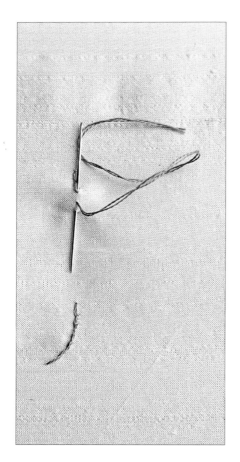

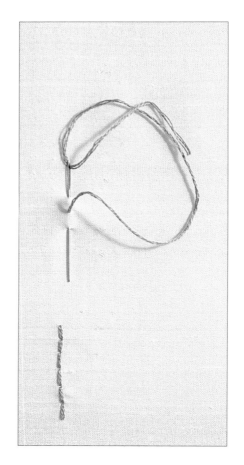

the fabric at the beginning of the placement for the stem or outline and work one single straight stitch. Bring the needle up again half a stitch length away in the direction of and exactly on the line of the stem. Take the needle down (working back on yourself) half way along the length of the first stitch and just to one side of it, then bring it back up half a stitch length further away.

2 Continue in this way until you reach the desired length of the stem or outline.

Back Stitch in Embroidery Floss ▶

Back stitch makes a continuous line useful for outlining or adding detail to a design.

1 Bring the needle up through your fabric a stitch length away from your required starting point in the direction of working and go back down into the fabric at the starting point. Bring the needle back up a stitch length away from the start of the first stitch exactly on the line being worked and take it back down again next to the

Stem Stitch in Embroidery Floss ▲

This is a very useful stitch not only for working stems to silk ribbon flowers but also for marking the outline of many shapes. You can curve the line of stitches (in any direction) or it can be worked straight.

1 Bring your needle up through

point where your first stitch emerged.

2 Continue in this way until you reach your required length of work.

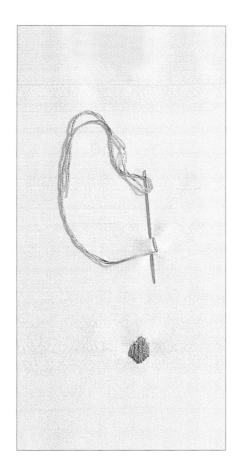

close to the end of the first stitch as possible.

2 Continue this way until you have filled the required area.

Double-edged Satin Rose ▶

Satin ribbon makes a three-dimensional rose which looks good either on its own or in a cluster. It is not easy to launder and so would not be used on clothing. To show up more clearly in the photograph, sewing thread in a contrasting colour has been used but you should, of course, use a matching colour to obscure the securing stitches.

Satin Stitch in Embroidery Floss ▲

Usually used to fill in an area with solid colour.

1 Bring the needle up through the fabric and take it down at the required length. Bring the needle up again as close to the start of the first stitch as possible, then take the needle back down again as

1 Take any width of double-edged satin ribbon. You will need about 50cm (20in) per rose. You will also need a length of matching thread in a sharp-pointed embroidery needle. Cut the end of the ribbon on the cross and fold it down. Roll the ribbon round three times to make a firm tube and stitch into place at the bottom. Holding the roll in your right hand and the rest of the ribbon in your left hand turn the ribbon back on itself and wrap it round

the roll in the right hand. Stitch into place.

2 Keep on folding the ribbon in the left hand and stitching it around the rose in the right hand, until you feel the rose is the correct size.

3 To finish off, cut the ribbon on the cross and tuck it back on itself. Stitch down, then sew into place on the fabric.

THE PROJECTS

$\mathcal{L}$AUREL WREATH CUSHION

This cushion is an ideal beginners' project worked on calico; a fabric which is very simple to handle and easy to embroider. I was inspired by the classical laurel leaf motif for the embroidery to finish the cushion with a gathered and knotted border as an echo of a Roman toga.

YOU WILL NEED:
90 cm (36 in) unbleached calico, 115cm (45in) wide
3m (3½yds) 7mm emerald green silk ribbon
embroidery hoop or frame
tailor's chalk or dressmaker's marking pencil
no. 18 chenille needle
crewel needle or similar
matching green embroidery floss
40cm (16in) cushion pad
matching sewing thread

diagonal stitch
ribbon stitch
French knot

To stitch the design

1 Calico is liable to shrink when washed, so it is best that you pre-wash the fabric. Since you will also want to launder the embroidery, soak the ribbon in cold, salted water before using. This will prevent the dye from running in any subsequent washes.

2 Press the fabric carefully ensuring that all the creases are [rem]oved, as you cannot iron over the embroidery once you have finished the piece.

3 Cut a square of calico, 43 x 43cm (17¼ x 17¼ in) and stretch in an embroidery hoop or frame. Mark the centre of your fabric with two crossed pins or a tailor's chalk cross.

4 Working from the centre, draw a circle 19cm (8in) in diameter with either a pencil or tailor's chalk. Mark the centre top and bottom of the circle with a vertical pin.

5 Using the green silk ribbon, bring the needle up through the fabric about 3cm (1¼in) to the left of the bottom centre pin. Lay the ribbon in a diagonal line of 7cm (2¾in), then take the needle down into the fabric, forming one diagonal straight stitch (do not pull the ribbon tight). Repeat this stitch,

this time bringing the needle up 3cm (1¼ in) to the right of the bottom centre pin. Lay the ribbon on top of the first stitch and take it to the back of the fabric to make the second diagonal stitch crossing over the first.

6 Starting 1cm (⅜ in) up the left-hand side (see stitch diagram on page 30), work pairs of ribbon

stitch leaves around the edge of the circle. As you work round the circle decrease the size of the leaves very slightly. Stop about 2cm (¾in) from the top centre pin, then work a single leaf at a slight angle to the pencil circle, pointing upwards.

7 Repeat step 6 to work all the way up the right-hand side of the circle.

NOTES AND TIPS

Do not worry about whether there is an equal number of leaf sets on either side of the wreath as this will not be noticeable. Be more concerned with forming the ribbon stitch leaves correctly.

8 To finish off the design, pin the two diagonal stitches at the bottom of the wreath, so that they curve a little to give the effect of a bow, then, using two strands of the embroidery floss, attach the ribbons to the fabric with evenly spaced French knots. Remove the pins as you work.

To make up the cushion

The cushion cover is slip stitched together and can be unpicked for laundering. A zip could be fitted if desired but this cushion is really intended to be decorative rather than hardwearing.

1 From the remaining calico, cut a piece 43cm (17¼ in) square.

2 Place the square on top of the embroidered piece with right sides together and machine stitch round the sides, taking 1.5cm (⅝in) seam allowance and leaving a gap in one side large enough to insert the cushion pad. Trim the corners and turn right side out. Do not bother to push out the corners, leave them rounded.

3 Insert the cushion pad and slip stitch the sides of the gap together.

4 From the remaining calico, make up a strip 20cm (8in) wide and the length of the circumference of the cushion plus an extra 65cm (26in). Make this piece into a tube by stitching down one long side with a 1.5cm (⅝in) seam, right sides together, then turning right side out.

5 Place one end of the tube just to the right of the bottom right-hand corner and pin to the cushion. Take the tube along to the bottom left-hand corner, then tie the tube into a loose knot, so that it sits on the corner (see diagram 1). Pin in place. Stitch the tube to the cushion matching seams, leaving the first 10cm (4in) unattached. Repeat the process on the next two corners stitching the tube down completely.

6 Make the fourth knot next to the third knot. Tuck one raw end of the tube inside the other, ensuring that the tube closely fits the final side of the cushion. Turn under a narrow hem on the visible raw end and slip stitch in position (see diagram 2). Work the fourth knot along the tube until it lies over the final corner, the join should then disappear into the knot. Stitch the remaining side of the tube down to the cushion.

VARIATION
If adding a zip insert it across the middle of the cushion cover back, allowing extra fabric for seams.

diagram 1

diagram 2

BARREL CUSHION

Barrel cushions always look so elegant on a sofa or a chaise longue. On this one I have worked an abstract design which will look good in any modern sitting room. This is a simple project suitable for a beginner. It can be stitched on a shop-bought cushion if preferred.

YOU WILL NEED:

I purchased barrel cushion
  including pad
or
a barrel cushion pad and enough
  fabric to cover the pad, see
  below (I have used a self-striped
  damask type fabric)
tailor's chalk or dressmaker's
  marking pencil
embroidery hoop or frame
no. 18 chenille needle
2.5m (2¾yds) 4mm ginger silk
  ribbon
2m (2¼yds) 4mm light olive
  green silk ribbon
2m (2¼yds) 4mm dark olive
  green silk ribbon
I skein ginger embroidery floss
matching sewing thread

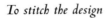

To stitch the design

1 For the cushion cover you will need three pieces of fabric, measured as follows:
* the length of the barrel cushion pad x the circumference plus 1.5cm (⅝ in) seam allowance all round;
* two circles the same size as the cushion pad ends plus seam allowances as before.

2 Working on the barrel of the cushion, measure 7.5cm (3in) from each end and draw a line in chalk or pencil. Stretch the fabric in a hoop or frame.

3 Because I was working on striped fabric I was able to work one pattern on each alternate stripe. If you choose to work on plain fabric then you just need to space each pattern equally at a distance of approximately 3cm (1¼in), being sure to keep clear of the seam allowances.

4 For each pattern, draw a 'V' shape which measures 3cm (1¼in) with the widest part approximately 2.25cm (1in) apart (see stitch diagram below).

⊸ couched straight stitch

◦ French knot

⊸ lazy daisy stitch

5 Using the ginger ribbon, work the 'V' shape in two long straight stitches.

6 Using the light olive ribbon, couch the ginger ribbon in two places at each side of the 'V' (only couch the ribbon loosely, so that the ginger ribbon stays straight).

7 Using the dark olive ribbon, work one French knot at the end of each ginger straight stitch.

8 With the same ribbon, work one lazy daisy stitch at the point of each 'V'.

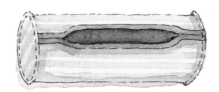

9 Work the opposite end of the barrel in the same way except you can, like me, reverse the direction of the 'V's if you prefer.

10 To work the ends of the cushion, find the centre and mark it with crossed pins. Mark 4 'V' shapes the same size as previously worked on the barrel all with the points inwards. Leave a small gap in the very centre.

11 Work the four 'V's in the same way as before without the lazy daisy stitch at the points.

12 Using the embroidery floss, make a very simple tassel (see page 13) and stitch it into the centre of the four 'V's.

To make up the cushion

1 Fold the piece for the barrel of the cushion in half lengthways, right sides together, and pin the long edge. Machine stitch for 5cm (2in) at either end of this edge, taking a 1.5cm (⅝in) seam allowance, thus leaving a gap large enough to insert the cushion pad.

2 Press the seam and the raw edges flat.

3 Pin one of the circle ends to the short edge of the barrel piece, with right sides together and raw edges aligned. Tack, then machine stitch all round with the usual seam allowance.

4 Repeat at the other end (see diagram). Turn right side out. Insert the cushion pad, then slip stitch the gap together by hand.

ℒACY BED CUSHION

Scattering a selection of small cushions on your bed always gives it a more luxurious and enticing look. This small square cushion can be easily made with a knowledge of only three stitches. It uses double-edged satin ribbon for the first time. While this is not suitable for the embroidered stitches, it is very good for making the twisted roses. They cannot be laundered but are particularly suitable for purely decorative pieces.

YOU WILL NEED:
a purchased white cotton or silk
   cushion
or
a 30cm (12in) square cushion
   pad and 50cm (½yd) white
   cotton sheeting fabric, 165cm
   (64in) wide, plus enough lace
   in length to go round the
   cushion twice
tailor's chalk or dressmaker's
   marking pencil
embroidery hoop or frame
no. 18 chenille needle
crewel needle or similar
light green embroidery floss

1.5m (1⅔yds) 9mm double-
   edged dark pink satin ribbon
dark pink sewing thread (to
   match satin ribbon)
1.5m (1⅔yds) 7mm light
   green silk ribbon
white sewing thread

To stitch the design

1 If making your own cushion, cut two squares of sheeting, both measuring 33cm (13in) per side. Using chalk or pencil, mark a 30cm (12in) square centrally on the right side of one of the squares. Draw a diagonal line from corner to corner of the marked square. Repeat to make a diagonal in the opposite direction. Next draw a

series of lines, parallel to each diagonal, each line to be 4.5cm (1¾ in) away from the last. Work out to the corners of the square, so that the whole of the marked area is covered in a lattice.

2 If you are working with a purchased cushion cover, draw the lattice on one side as described in step 1, taking the lines right up to the edges.

3 Stretch the marked square in an embroidery hoop or frame. Using two strands of the green embroidery floss, work all the lattice pattern in stem stitch. Try to keep your stitches as even and straight as possible.

4 With the dark pink satin ribbon, make thirteen double-edged satin roses.

5 Stitch the roses securely onto the lattice in the positions shown in the photograph below.

6 Using the green silk ribbon, work ribbon stitch and side ribbon stitch leaves around the roses. Vary the number of leaves and the positions with each rose.

To make up the cushion

1 Join the lace into a circle by stitching the two short ends, right sides together, with a 1cm (³⁄₈in) seam.

2 Gather the lace to half its original length along the top of the straight edge. Place on top of the embroidered square, with right sides together, so that the gathered line of the lace lies on top of the marked stitching line. Pin in place, adjusting the gathers so that they lie evenly but with extra fullness at the corners (see diagram). Tack in place and remove pins.

3 Place the second square of cotton sheeting on top of the embroidered piece with right sides together and machine stitch round the sides, taking 1.5cm (⁵⁄₈in) seam allowance and leaving a gap in one side large enough to insert the cushion pad. Trim the corners and turn right side out.

4 Insert the cushion pad and slip stitch the sides of the gap together.

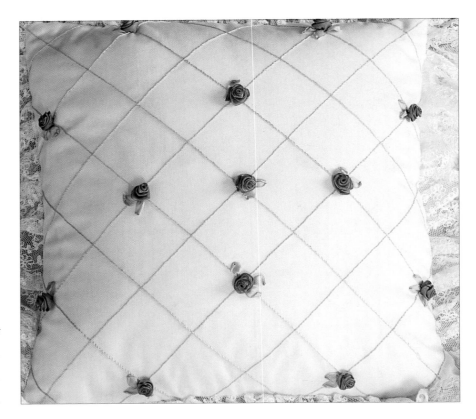

HEART-SHAPED BED PILLOW

Small pillows placed at the top of a bed can really add style and elegance to a bed. This small heart-shaped pillow is fairly simple to work yet looks quite involved to the untrained eye.

YOU WILL NEED:

Im (Iyd) pink silk dupion, 115cm (45in) wide

tailor's chalk or dressmaker's marking pencil

embroidery hoop or frame

no. 18 chenille needle

crewel needle or similar

light pink embroidery floss

50cm (20in) 4mm dark pink silk ribbon

50cm (20in) 4mm medium pink silk ribbon

50cm (20in) 4mm light pink silk ribbon

light green embroidery floss

75cm (30in) 4mm mauve silk ribbon

lemon yellow embroidery floss

50cm (20in) 4mm lavender silk ribbon

50cm (20in) 7mm dusty pink silk ribbon

gold embroidery floss

50cm (20in) 7mm light green silk ribbon

50cm (20in) 4mm dark green silk ribbon

dark green embroidery floss

50cm (20in) 4mm light green silk ribbon

heart-shaped pillow pad

To stitch the design

I Cut out two pieces of silk dupion, 30cm (12in) square, then draw the shape of the embroidery using the template on page 43 onto the centre of one of the squares using tailor's chalk or pencil. Stretch the fabric into a hoop or frame.

2 Starting at the bottom, work three spider's web roses in the position shown in the stitch diagram on page 42 as follows. Using two strands of light pink embroidery floss, work the web. Change to the dark pink ribbon, work two rounds of the web and fasten off. Next work three rounds in medium pink, then finally two loose rounds in the light pink.

3 Work the buds in medium pink using two side ribbon stitches back to back, then work the calyxes. Using the light green embroidery floss, first work a fly stitch round each bud, then a single straight stitch from the middle of each bud to its base and finally a long straight stitch for the stalk.

4 Work all the tiny mauve flowers in small loop stitches, making three petals to each flower. Work the centres in French knots using two strands of lemon yellow embroidery floss.

5 Work the little lavender flowers in ribbon stitch and side ribbon stitch (see the note on page 18).

6 Work the dog roses in 7mm dusty pink ribbon each with five petals in ribbon stitch. The rosebuds are also worked in ribbon stitch. There is a French knot in the middle and pistil stitches on each petal, all worked in two strands of gold embroidery floss.

7 Work the leaves to the spider's web roses using the 7mm light green ribbon in both ribbon stitch and side ribbon stitch.

8 Work the leaves to the lavender flowers in 4mm dark green ribbon in ribbon stitch.

⬭	side ribbon stitch
⬮	ribbon stitch
〜〜〜	stem stitch
꞊∕꞊	whipped running stitch
—○	pistil stitch
▽	loop stitch
⊙	French knot
⅄	fly stitch and straight stitch
✺	spider's web rose

9 Work the stems to the lavender flowers using two strands of matching dark green embroidery floss and stem stitch with one or two straight stitches to attach the petals to the stem.

10 The final stage is to join up all the flower groups using light green 4mm silk ribbon and working in whipped running stitch.

To make up the cushion

1 Cut the two squares of fabric into heart shapes, using the cushion pad as a guide and adding a 2.5cm (1in) seam allowance.

2 From the remaining silk fabric cut strips 15cm (6in) wide and as long as possible. Join at the short edges to make one long strip.

3 Fold this strip in half length-ways, then pin it to the right side of the embroidered piece, raw edges matching and making small pleats as you go (see diagram). About 10cm (4in) from the end, cut the strip to the right length,

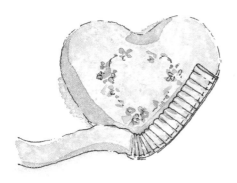

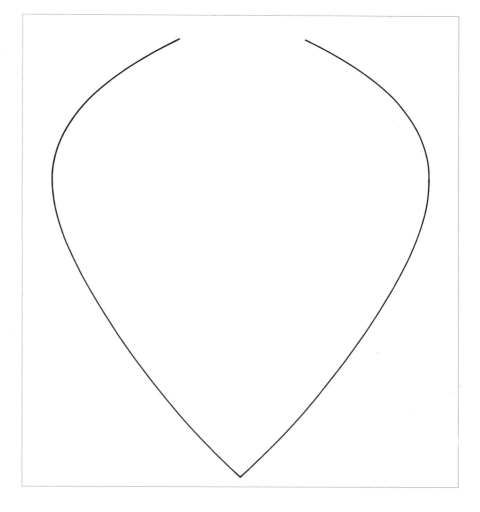

then open out and stitch to the start of the strip, right sides together. Finish pleating. Tack, then machine stitch in place.

4 Place the remaining heart-shaped piece of fabric on top of the embroidered piece, right sides together and with the edging

still facing inwards. Pin, tack, then machine stitch over the previous stitching line, leaving a gap large enough to insert the cushion pad.

5 Turn right side out and pull out the pleated edging. Insert the pad, then slip stitch the edges of the gap together.

THAI SILK CUSHION

This beautiful Thai silk cushion instantly caught my eye in a department store and I fell in love with the colour and the fabric. I just knew I could work a design that would look great on this background. I started out with a simple bouquet design in mind but the idea gradually developed into this rather ornate urn filled with all kinds of flowers. This is a project for the more advanced silk ribbon embroiderer.

YOU WILL NEED:
Thai silk cushion (pad included),
   40cm (16in) square
tailor's chalk or dressmaker's
   marking pencil
embroidery hoop or frame
no. 18 chenille needle
crewel needle or similar
75cm (30in) 4mm light lavender
   silk ribbon
75cm (30in) 4mm dark lavender
   silk ribbon
50cm (20in) 7mm medium
   lavender silk ribbon
50cm (20in) 7mm pale green
   silk ribbon
3m (3½ yds) 4mm dusty pink
   silk ribbon
3m (3½yds) 4mm light dusty
   pink silk ribbon
1m (40in) 7mm cerise silk
   ribbon

1m (40in) 4mm cream silk
   ribbon
2m (2¼yds) 4mm light pink
   silk ribbon
3m (3½yds) 4mm mustard
   silk ribbon
3m (3½yds) 4mm lemon silk
   ribbon
1m (40in) 4mm dark turquoise
   silk ribbon
2m (2¼yds) 4mm light turquoise
   silk ribbon
1m (40in) 4mm lemon/green
   silk ribbon
1m (40in) 4mm pale moss green
   silk ribbon
50cm (20in) 4mm dark green
   silk ribbon
2m (2¼yds) 4mm moss green
   silk ribbon
pale brown embroidery floss for
   foliage stalks
pale green embroidery floss for
   rose and peony stems

green embroidery floss for
   rosebud calyxes and stems
1 piece of bronze silk dupion,
   11 x 13cm (4½ x 5½in)
bronze sewing thread
gold embroidery thread
1 brass cherub (see page 128)
clear varnish
fabric glue
hot glue gun (optional)

To stitch the design

I Mark the positions of all the main flowers, stems and the urn on the centre of the cushion front using tailor's chalk or pencil and following the full size stitch diagram on page 48 and the template on page 49. Stretch the fabric in a hoop or frame.

2 Work the three peonies first. Using the light lavender ribbon, work one long lazy daisy stitch for the centre of the flower, then four or five ribbon stitches at the sides. Change to the dark lavender ribbon and work four or five twisted pistil stitches radiating out from the centre. Next using the 7mm medium lavender ribbon, work six ribbon stitches fanning out downwards and to the sides, then infill with ribbon stitch leaves in pale green ribbon.

3 Using the dusty and light dusty pink ribbon, work the two lilacs next in French knots. Mix the two colours randomly to give the flowers a shaded look.

4 Using the 7mm cerise ribbon, work the buds using ribbon stitch and side ribbon stitch.

5 Using the cream ribbon, work one lazy daisy stitch for the centre of each of the four roses with one side ribbon stitch on either side. Using the light pink ribbon, work two ribbon stitches at either side of the cream stitches, then one stitch slanting downwards.

6 Sew the five mustard flowers by starting with three French knots in mustard ribbon for the centres. Using the lemon ribbon, work twice round the knots in coral stitch, then once round the outside with the mustard ribbon, again in coral stitch.

7 To work the seven turquoise flowers, first work the centres with three French knots in the dark turquoise, then work round the knots with the light turquoise in lazy daisy stitches.

8 Using the lemon/green ribbon, work the foliage branches in ribbon and side ribbon stitches. Repeat for the leaves on the rose stalks using pale moss green ribbon.

9 Work all the remaining leaves on the flowers as follows: rosebud leaves in pale moss green ribbon in ribbon stitch; mustard flower leaves in dark green ribbon and ribbon stitch; two leaves on the left-hand peony stalk in 7mm pale green ribbon and ribbon stitch and the leaves for the turquoise flowers in moss green ribbon worked in lazy daisy stitch.

10 Work all the stalks in stem stitch using two strands of embroidery floss as in the list of materials, except the stalks and calyxes for the cerise buds. To work these, using two strands of embroidery floss, first work a fly stitch round each bud, then a single straight stitch from the middle of each bud to its base and finally a long straight stitch for the stalk.

11 Transfer the outline of the urn given in the template to the bronze silk using chalk or pencil. Machine stitch all round the outline, then cut round the shape 1cm ($^3/_8$ in) outside the line of stitching.

12 Turn back the allowance beyond the stitched line, so that the stitching cannot be seen from the front. Snip where necessary, so that the turnings lie flat. Press.

13 Pin the urn in position on the cushion front and slip stitch to the cushion using tiny stitches. Remove the pins.

14 Work all round the outline of the urn in stem stitch using three strands of gold thread.

ROSEBUD

ribbon stitch

side ribbon stitch

PEONY

lazy daisy stitch

ribbon stitch

pistil stitch

LILAC

   French knot

ROSE

lazy daisy stitch

side ribbon stitch

ribbon stitch

MUSTARD FLOWER

French knot

coral stitch

TURQUOISE FLOWER

French knot

lazy daisy stitch

FOLIAGE BRANCHES

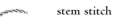   ribbon stitch

side ribbon stitch

stem stitch

   lazy daisy stitch

fly stitch and
straight stitch

Work a double row at the top and bottom of the urn about 4mm (1/6 in) apart. Fill in the space between these two rows with diagonal straight stitches.

15 In order to prevent the brass cherub from tarnishing, wash it in soapy water, dry, then seal the surface with a clear varnish. Stick the cherub in position on the urn using fabric glue. A hot glue gun is good for this job.

$\mathscr{P}$ILLOW CASE & SHEET

I have always loved beautiful bed linen. This book provided the opportunity for me to design some linen that would be wonderful to use when guests come to stay. The materials given will embroider a single bed set.

YOU WILL NEED:

1.5m (1²/₃ yds) 4mm dark pink silk ribbon

Im (40in) 4mm medium pink silk ribbon

2.5m (2³/₄ yds) 4mm light pink silk ribbon

1.5m (1²/₃ yds) 7mm medium pink silk ribbon

variegated green coton perlé

Im (40in) 7mm light green silk ribbon

2.2m (2¹/₂ yds) 7mm pink Mokuba ribbon

pink embroidery floss (to match Mokuba ribbon)

tailor's chalk or dressmaker's marking pencil

purchased pillow case and single sheet in cotton or linen

embroidery hoop or frame

no. 18 chenille needle

crewel needle or similar

To stitch the pillowcase

1 Since you will want to launder the embroidered bed linen, soak the ribbons in cold, salted water before using. This will prevent the dye from running in any subsequent washes.

2 Draw the design onto the top left-hand corner of the pillowcase following the stem shapes shown in the stitch diagram on page 52 and using tailor's chalk or pencil. Stretch this area in an embroidery hoop or frame.

3 Using the three shades of 4mm pink ribbon, work the three bullion roses in the positions shown in the stitch diagram.

4 Next work the outer petals of the bullion roses in ribbon stitch using the 7mm medium pink ribbon.

5 Using the same colour, work the large buds in ribbon stitch and side ribbon stitch.

6 Work two sprays of buds in light pink in ribbon stitch and one in dark pink.

7 Next mark the place where the bow will cross the stems with a pin, which will give you a point at which to bring the stems together, then stitch the eight stems in stem stitch using the variegated green coton perlé.

8 Using the same coton perlé to match the stems, work round the buds in fly stitch with a straight stitch from the base of the bud to the centre on some of the buds.

9 Using the 7mm light green ribbon, work the leaves around the flowers of the bullion roses and down the stem in both ribbon stitch and side ribbon stitch.

10 Using the Mokuba ribbon, bring the needle up through the pillow case at a point approximately 12cm (4½in) below the lowest left-hand flower bud, then lay the ribbon in a bow on the pillowcase, crossing the stems at their narrowest point. Add twists and turns into the long tails and pin in place, then take the ribbon to the back of the case approximately 12cm (4½in) to the right of the furthest right-hand large bud.

11 Finish off carefully at the back. Attach the ribbon to the fabric along its length with French knots made using two strands of matching embroidery floss and spacing them about 1cm (³⁄₈ in) apart.

To stitch the sheet

Work the design onto the sheet in exactly the same way, the only difference is that the bow tails will take different twists and turns. Position the design just below the top large hem in the centre. The bow is nearest to the hem with the flowers pointing away from it, so that the design will be the right way up when the linen is on the bed.

⅄	fly stitch and straight stitch
⟿	bullion stitch
⬯	ribbon stitch
⟋⟍	stem stitch
◉	French knot

PELMET & TIEBACKS

Damask is an ideal fabric for curtains and perfectly suitable for silk ribbon embroidery. For this design I wanted to add just a little colour to reflect the colours and style in the room. The abstract design evolved from the triangular design of the pelmet and tie-backs and is loosely reminiscent of a jester juggling. This pelmet fits flush into a recess. It's a simple project, highly suitable for a beginner, consisting of just three stitches in a straightforward combination.

YOU WILL NEED:

stiffened stick-on pelmet backing
   (see method)
damask fabric, or your own
   choice (see method)
embroidery hoop or frame
no. 18 chenille needle
approximately 2m (2¼yds) 7mm
   Mokuba variegated sylk ribbon
   colour 001
approximately 1m (40in) 3.5mm
   Mokuba variegated sylk ribbon
   colour 001
fabric glue and brush
purchased tassels (one for each
   point of the pelmet, see below)
sewing thread
4 curtain rings

To stitch the pelmet

1 The number of triangles required depends on the length of your pelmet. Measure your window frame and divide by 24.5cm (9½in) to find the number you will need. One of these will be made up of two half triangles (for each end of the pelmet). If the required width does not divide exactly, you can adjust the number of triangles and/or the length of the overlap (see diagram 1, page 57). If the amount left over is more than 12.5cm (5in), add an extra triangle and increase the length of the overlap. If it is under 12.5cm (5in), just reduce the length of the overlap.

2 Make a pattern for the triangles from the template on page 54, measuring 35.5cm (14in) across and 35.5cm (14in) long.

3 Cut the required number of triangles out of stiffened pelmet fabric. Cut one in half through the vertical centre line. Cut the same number of fabric triangles but allowing an additional 1.5cm (⅝in) seam allowance all round.

4 Starting 13.5cm (5¼in) up from the bottom point of the first full triangle for the pelmet, mark the centre of the fabric with a pin. Stretch the fabric in an embroidery hoop or frame.

5 Using the 7mm width variegated ribbon, work three ribbon stitches each 2cm (¾in) long radiating out from the point marked by the pin as shown in the close-up photograph on page 56. Next work a short horizontal straight stitch directly under the three previously worked stitches.

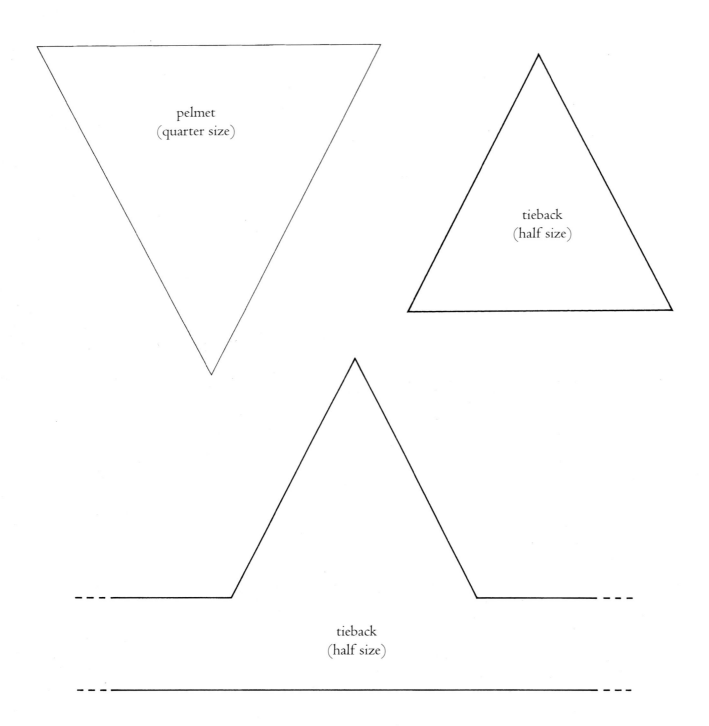

pelmet
(quarter size)

tieback
(half size)

tieback
(half size)

6 Work a French knot directly underneath, then a French knot at the tip of the two side stitches and two above the middle stitch. Repeat in the same position on the point of each full triangle.

7 On the half triangles at each end of the pelmet, work the centre ribbon stitch in 3.5mm width ribbon and just one ribbon stitch either to the left or to the right depending on whether this is the left or right-hand half triangle.

NOTES AND TIPS

The secret with this design is to be selective about the lengths of ribbon cut from the variegated reel, so that you work the right colours in the appropriate places.

To stitch the tiebacks

1 Measure the length of tieback required by placing a tape measure round the curtain at the required height and to the required fullness. Cut out a piece of stiffened pelmet backing to this length and 5cm (2in) wide with a triangle point in the centre, following the template. Cut a triangle using the tieback template. Cut the same shapes in fabric, two of each, adding seam allowances as before.

2 Work the tiebacks in exactly the same way as the pelmet but using the 3.5mm width ribbon throughout. The base of the ribbon stitch is 11cm (4¼in) up from the point on the large triangle and 9cm (3½in) up on the small one.

To make up the pelmet

1 Place one of the pelmet backing triangles centrally on the reverse of the embroidered triangle and press firmly.

2 Fold back the seam allowance of the fabric and press down, folding in the corner of the point neatly. Use a little glue to hold the fabric down or secure with a few stitches if necessary. Repeat with the other triangles.

3 Lay out the triangles in a row, with a half triangle at each end.

Every alternate triangle is placed behind the ones on either side, starting with the half triangles underneath, so that there is an 11cm (4½in) overlap (see diagram 1). Mark the points of the overlaps with pins, apply glue to the overlapping area on the underneath triangles, then stick down.

4 Stick or stitch tassels to the point of each triangle.

5 Cut a piece of pelmet backing to the exact length of the pelmet and 10cm (4in) deep. Lay the length of embroidered triangles on top. Press until firmly stuck.

6 Fix a pelmet board to the window. Apply glue to the

35,5 cm   24,5 cm   11 cm

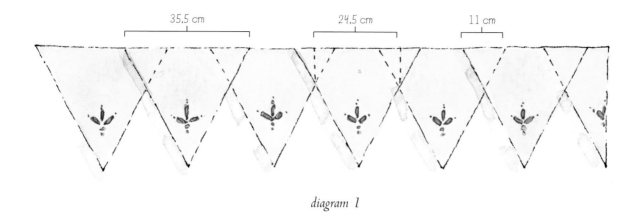

diagram 1

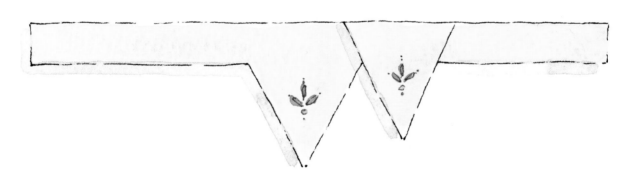

diagram 2

uppermost side of the board and press the pelmet in position.

To make up the tiebacks

1 Stick the stiffened pelmet backing to the fabric for the tieback and for the triangles, folding the fabric to the back in the same way as for the pelmet. Stick one triangle to each tieback as shown in diagram 2.

2 Stitch curtain rings to the back of the tieback at each end. Fix wall hooks at the desired height.

TABLECLOTH & NAPKINS

*Summer afternoon teas look wonderful when served on fresh crisp table linen. I have worked a bold abstract design on a
lovely lemon yellow cotton chintz for this project. The tablecloth would also look very pretty as the overcloth
on a round occasional table picking out the colour from a print floor length cloth underneath. This quantity of fabric
is enough for the cloth and two napkins.*

YOU WILL NEED:

3m (3½yds) 7mm purple silk
   ribbon

1.5m (1²/₃yds) 4mm pale
   lavender silk ribbon

2.5m (2¾yds) 4mm turquoise
   silk ribbon

4m (4yds) 4mm pale green silk
   ribbon

1.6m (1¾yds) lemon yellow
   cotton chintz fabric, 115cm
   (45in) wide

lemon yellow sewing thread

no. 18 chenille needle

13cm (5in) embroidery hoop

To stitch and make up the design

1 Since you will want to launder
the table linen, soak the ribbon
in cold, salted water before using.
This will prevent the dye from running in any subsequent washes.

2 Cut one square 115cm (45in)
wide for the tablecloth and two
45cm (17½in) squares for the napkins from the remainder.

3 Turn under a narrow hem 1cm
(³/₈ in) wide on the large square
and press, then turn under the same
amount again and press to create a
double hem. Machine stitch in
place. Repeat on both the squares
for the napkins.

4 Work the design shown in the
photograph on page 60 in all
four corners of the tablecloth and
one corner on each napkin as follows: stretch one corner of the fabric onto the hoop, there should be a
border of approximately 2.5cm
(1in) overhanging the hoop. Using
the purple ribbon, work one large
lazy daisy stitch in the centre of the
stretched fabric.

5 Taking the same ribbon, work
three or four long twisted
straight stitches. To do this, twist
the ribbon after you have pulled it
through to the front, then take the
needle to the back of the fabric,
leaving a loose stitch at the front.
The end of the stitch will form a
spiral curl and the way the ribbon
curls will determine whether you
have space for three or four stitches.

6 Changing to the pale lavender
ribbon, work three more long,
twisted, straight stitches. Now

using the turquoise ribbon, work three more long, twisted, straight stitches.

7 Still using the turquoise ribbon, work approximately five or six loop stitches in the middle of the shape.

8 Using the green ribbon, add five twisted ribbon stitch leaves to the bottom of the design. Work the stitch as described on page 17 but put a single twist in the ribbon.

9 Still using the green ribbon, work lazy daisy leaves around the bottom of the design as shown.

NOTES AND TIPS

Twist the ribbon many times to get it to curl but do not twist too tightly or the fronds will be too thin.

CALICO HAT

I spotted this delightful calico hat at a craft fair and instantly fell in love with it. The hat lent itself to my design which can be worked in any combination of colours; perhaps you would like to work it in primary colours mixing and matching the loop colours with the knot colours?

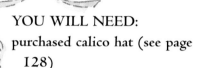

YOU WILL NEED:
purchased calico hat (see page 128)
13cm (5in) embroidery hoop
no. 18 chenille needle
3m (3½yds) 4mm tan silk ribbon
3m (3½yds) 4mm black silk ribbon

To stitch the design

1 If the hat is lined, as mine was, you will need to unpick the crown lining before you start, so that the back of the work is not exposed on the inside of the hat.

2 Using the embroidery hoop, stretch a section of the hat. (I started at the centre back and worked to the left.)

3 This simple stitch is a kind of crossed lazy daisy anchored by a French knot. Starting with the tan ribbon, work the stitch as shown in the diagram below, bringing the needle up at A and down at B, then up again at C and down at D. The stitch is about 13mm (½in) high.

4 Place a pin through the ribbons at the point where they cross over (E). Change to the black ribbon, bring the needle up at E and work a French knot.

5 Work a second pattern stitch in the same way as the first, leaving about 5mm (¼ in) between the two stitches.

6 Change the colours so that the crossed lazy daisy is worked in black and the French knot in tan. Work two stitches, then change back to the original colourway.

7 Change the colour combination every two pattern stitches.

8 Work all around the hat, moving the embroidery hoop along as you progress. Continue until you meet up with the first stitch.

9 When you have finished your embroidery, slip stitch the lining back into place in the crown of the hat.

VARIATION

You could easily work this design on a ribbon to make a hat band as in the following project. Use a grosgrain ribbon or even an edged strip of fabric.

Other applications for this design might be round the collar of a blouse or on the edge of a pocket.

NOTES AND TIPS

After every four or five stitches, it is a good idea to measure the last stitch to make sure you're keeping to the correct size, rather than gradually scaling up or down.

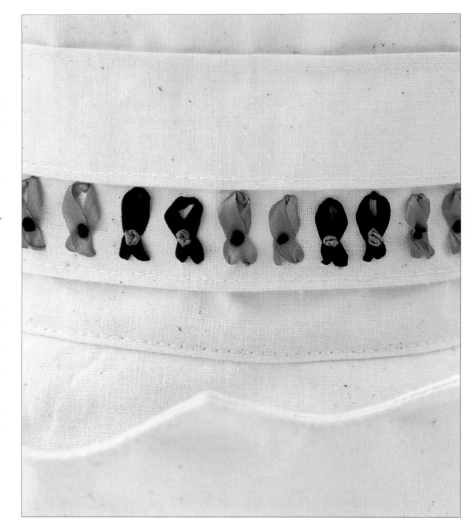

SUNFLOWER HAT BAND

Sunflowers are always popular. They have a simple, summery look about them which makes them a perfect design to decorate a straw hat. This embroidery is worked on double wire-edged ribbon, which is easily tied into a flamboyant bow. The design is made up of fully open sunflowers and buds in varying positions. Some have stems, some don't: it's up to you.

YOU WILL NEED:

1.5m (1²/₃yds) green double wire-edged Thai silk ribbon, 4cm (1¹/₂in) wide

purchased straw hat

13mm (5in) embroidery hoop

no. 18 chenille needle

crewel needle or similar

1.3m (1¹/₂yds) 4mm brown silk ribbon

1.5m (1²/₃yds) 4mm orange silk ribbon

2.8m (3yds) 7mm yellow silk ribbon

1m (40in) 13mm green silk ribbon

50cm (20in) 7mm green silk ribbon

matching green embroidery floss

To stitch the design

I Tie the wire-edged ribbon around the hat making a full bow at one side. Trim the ends into a 'V' shape. With pins mark the centre front and back of the hat on the ribbon.

2 Leaving the ribbon tied in a bow, carefully remove it from the hat and stretch it in the embroidery hoop. Start stitching at the pin marking the centre front and work your first whole sunflower in the middle of the band as described in the following steps.

3 Using brown ribbon, work one French knot surrounded by a circle of French knots. Change to orange ribbon and work a second circle of French knots. Using the yellow ribbon, work petals in ribbon stitch all round the circle of French knots.

4 Using the 13mm green ribbon, work leaves in ribbon stitch randomly below the flower head. You could also add some smaller leaves using the 7mm green ribbon. Stitch the stem using two strands of embroidery floss and working in stem stitch.

5 Work a half-open bud on either side as follows: stitch a central French knot in brown with three or four others in a half circle close to it. Add a second half circle in orange, then five or six ribbon stitch petals radiating out from the French knots. Add a leaf in 13mm green ribbon and a stem as before.

6 Work a closed bud to the left of the flowers already stitched as follows: using yellow ribbon, work two back-to-back ribbon stitches, then a straight stitch in green ribbon underneath and below that one or two ribbon stitch leaves

in 13mm green ribbon and a stem as before.

7 The stitch diagram below shows the three variations described above in a suggested arrangement. Follow this until your wire-edged ribbon is full, or just work your own pattern of flowers.

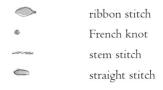

	ribbon stitch
	French knot
	stem stitch
	straight stitch

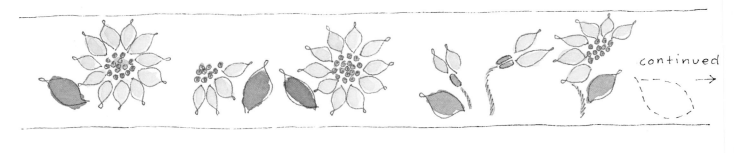

continued ----→

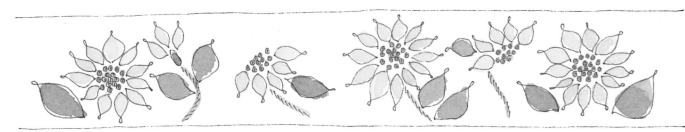

CHINESE LINEN BLOUSE

For this Chinese style blouse, I've chosen a classic design, which never goes out of fashion. The blouse provided me with a theme for the motif, which is reminiscent of the blue-and-white Willow pattern on china. Even a small amount of embroidery will personalise a purchased blouse. The design I have used is not too fussy so that the blouse could be worn with jeans or dressed up to wear in the evening.

YOU WILL NEED:

50cm (20in) 4mm medium blue silk ribbon

50cm (20in) 4mm light blue silk ribbon

25cm (10in) 7mm dusty blue silk ribbon

dark grey embroidery floss

25cm (10in) 4mm very dark blue/purple silk ribbon

50cm (20in) 4mm dark blue silk ribbon

purchased blouse

tailor's chalk or dressmaker's marking pencil

13cm (5in) embroidery hoop

no. 18 chenille needle

crewel needle or similar

To stitch the design

1 Since you will want to launder the embroidery, soak the ribbon in cold, salted water before using. This will prevent the dye from running in any subsequent washes.

2 Mark the position of the bird and the flower onto the blouse with tailor's chalk or pencil, following the outline of the full size stitch diagram below.

3 Stretch the area to be worked into the embroidery hoop.

⬭	straight stitch (ribbon)
◦	French knot
⬯	ribbon stitch
⬰	side ribbon stitch
⎼⎼⎼	stem stitch
—	straight stitch (floss)

4 Following the ribbon colours in the diagram, work the main left-hand part of the wing first with a single straight stitch, then the small feathers up the right-hand side of the wing also in straight stitch, varying their length and fanning them out towards the top.

5 Next stitch the body, then the tail feathers and the head, all in straight stitch.

6 Using two strands of the embroidery floss, work a straight stitch for the beak and a French knot for the eye.

7 Work the flower by starting with two small straight stitches in the very dark blue/purple ribbon, then work four petals in the 7mm ribbon using ribbon stitch: the two outermost petals give the flower head a better shape if they are worked in side ribbon stitch.

8 Work three petals in between the four just worked in ribbon stitch using the dark blue ribbon.

9 To finish, change to two strands of the embroidery floss and work the stem in stem stitch, then the stamen in straight stitch.

NOTES AND TIPS

Try the blouse on in order to mark the best position for the embroidery, no two people are the same shape or size.

The design could also be worked on a waistcoat or jacket.

ℰVENING WRAP

I had an idea in mind that I wanted to produce a very luxurious evening wrap. Not an everyday useful item, but an item that in years to come will be found in a drawer and mused upon. A 'what was it worn for and by whom' garment. The ribbon colours tone with the silk fabric creating a rich but subtle decoration at either end of the wrap.

YOU WILL NEED:

1m (1yd) metallic shot silk fabric

2m (2yds) lining fabric

matching sewing thread for beads and fabric

20cm (8in) embroidery hoop or frame

no. 18 chenille needle

2m (2¼yds) Mokuba 7mm luminous moss green ribbon

sewing thread to match moss green Mokuba

6m (6½yds) Mokuba 7mm raysheen dark green ribbon

6m (6½yds) Mokuba 9mm metallic green organdie ribbon

1 2.25g packet antique glass beads

beading needle

To stitch the design

1 Cut the metallic silk fabric in half lengthwise, then machine stitch the two pieces together to make one long scarf shape. Trim and neaten the seam edges.

2 Cut the lining in two crosswise, then cut and join each piece as for the metallic silk to make two lengths of lining.

3 Place the metallic silk on top of one of the lining pieces, with wrong sides together. Machine stitch the two layers together round all four sides 13mm (½in) away from the edge. You are now going to treat the two fabrics as one and embroider through both. The lining gives stability to the silk.

4 With a pin, mark the centre of the width of the silk fabric

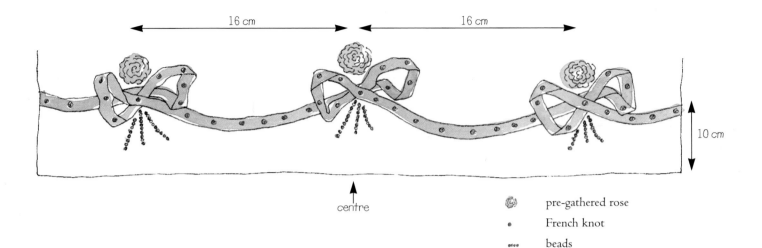

centre

pre-gathered rose

French knot

beads

10cm (4in) from one short edge. Stretch this area of the fabric in a hoop or frame.

5 Using the luminous ribbon, work three pre-gathered roses and stitch them onto the fabric as shown in the diagram above.

6 Change to the raysheen ribbon and lay it onto the fabric as shown. Pin into position, taking the ends of this ribbon beyond the machine stitched line.

7 Using the organdie ribbon, work French knots at regular intervals to secure the raysheen ribbon to the fabric, removing the pins as you go.

8 Stitch the beads using the beading needle onto the fabric to make three tails under each bow. There are approximately twelve beads in each tail.

9 Repeat steps 4 to 8 at the other end of the wrap.

To make up the wrap

1 Take the second piece of the lining fabric and place on top of the embroidered pieces, right sides together. Stitch all round the sides of the wrap trapping the ends of the raysheen ribbon as you do so. Take a 1.5cm (⅝in) seam allowance and leave a short 15cm (6in) gap on one long side.

2 Turn the wrap right side out through the gap, then hand stitch the sides of the gap together.

NOTES AND TIPS

Try to space the French knots at an equal distance apart along the raysheen ribbon. Stitch each of the bead tails in a slightly different direction and to varying lengths to add interest to the design.

EVENING WAISTCOAT

I have yearned for some time to design some elegant evening wear. This attractive waistcoat and the wrap on page 71 are the result. The waistcoat is very simple to work using only one basic silk ribbon stitch. You could work this design on any shop-bought or home-made waistcoat. Like the wrap, the ribbon colours tone with the silk fabric producing a rich but understated decoration.

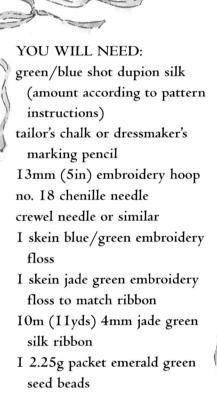

YOU WILL NEED:
green/blue shot dupion silk
   (amount according to pattern
   instructions)
tailor's chalk or dressmaker's
   marking pencil
13mm (5in) embroidery hoop
no. 18 chenille needle
crewel needle or similar
1 skein blue/green embroidery
   floss
1 skein jade green embroidery
   floss to match ribbon
10m (11yds) 4mm jade green
   silk ribbon
1 2.25g packet emerald green
   seed beads
beading needle
sewing thread to match beads

To stitch and make up the design

1 If you are making the waistcoat yourself, lay the pattern pieces on the fabric and either draw or tack round the shapes.

2 Using the full size stitch diagram on page 74, draw the design of the stalks and branches on the fabric shape for the right-hand waistcoat front, using either a pencil or tailor's chalk. Take the design to the shoulder of your waistcoat, ending the central stem with a curl. Note that the stalks are just curved lines and the branches for the berries are rather more curly at the ends. Be careful to avoid button or buttonhole placements.

3 Stretch the lower area of the design in the embroidery hoop. Note that you do not cut any of the fabric pieces until all the embroidery is completed. This is to make it easier to fit the narrow fronts in the hoop and to prevent fraying.

4 Using two strands of the blue/green embroidery floss, work the centre stalk of the design up the front of the waistcoat in stem stitch.

5 Work all the side stems using one strand of the jade green embroidery floss and working in stem stitch again.

6 Using the silk ribbon, work pairs of leaves on the side stems (follow the stitch diagram for position) in ribbon and side ribbon stitch as appropriate (see page 18).

7 Take the seed beads and, using the beading needle, stitch them

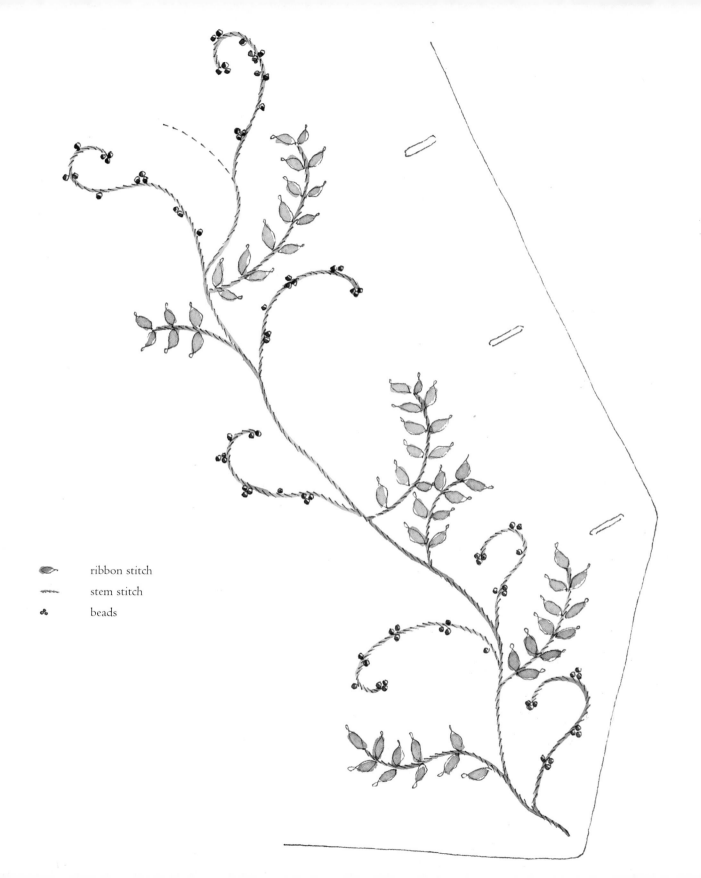

ribbon stitch

stem stitch

beads

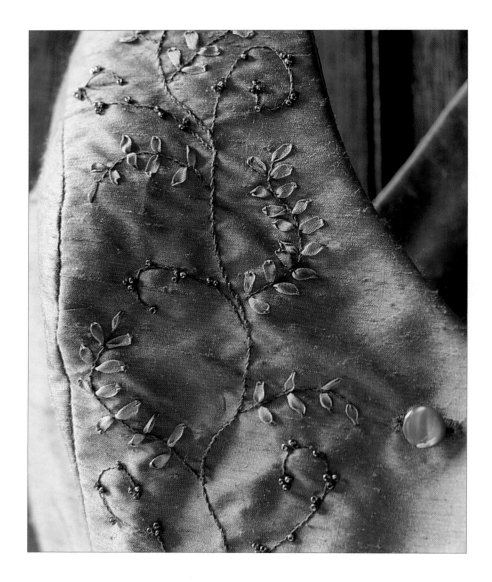

NOTES AND TIPS

I used only a small embroidery hoop, moving it up as I completed each segment of the design, which is easier than trying to stretch all the fabric for the whole design. Try to make both sides of the waistcoat if not identical, then balanced.

If working this design on a purchased waistcoat, remember to unpick the lining first, so that the back of the embroidery will be between the two layers.

onto the remaining stems either singly or in clusters of two or three.

8 Work the pattern in the same way on the left-hand front but making the design a mirror image.

Cut out all the pattern pieces and make up the waistcoat according to the pattern instructions.

THE PROJECTS

$\mathscr{G}$IFT BOX

This is a simple little design set into the lid of a fabric-covered box, which makes a gift in itself but could also be used to contain a special memento from an important occasion, such as a wedding or a Christening.

YOU WILL NEED:

I piece of cream silk, 25 x 25cm
    (10 x 10in), for the lid inset
tailor's chalk or dressmaker's
    marking pencil
13cm (5in) embroidery hoop
no. 18 chenille needle
crewel needle or similar
Im (40in) 7mm pale green silk
    ribbon
pale pink embroidery floss to
    tone with the pink ribbon
50cm (20in) 4mm pale lemon
    silk ribbon
50cm (20in) 4mm pale pink silk
    ribbon
green embroidery floss to tone
    with the green ribbon
card or template plastic
sharp craft knife
stiff card, approximately 3mm
    (1/8 in) thick
I piece of felt, 43 x 26cm
    (17 x 10in)

I piece of lemon yellow silk,
    46 x 30cm (18 x 12in), for
    the outside of the box
fabric glue and narrow glue
    brush
lemon yellow sewing thread
curved needle
I piece of lining (I used cream
    silk) 30 x 30cm (12 x 12in)
I circle of wadding, 8cm (3in)
    in diameter
30cm (12in) pearl beading or
    narrow decorative cord

To stitch the design

1 Mark a circle approximately 8cm (3in) in diameter in the centre of the piece of cream silk fabric for the lid inset using chalk or pencil. Stretch the fabric in the embroidery hoop.

2 Following the stitch diagram on page 78 and using green silk ribbon, start in the centre of the circle and work a Merrilyn bow. Do not take the bow nearer than 1cm (3/8 in) to the edge of the circle. Twist the tails to add interest.

3 Using two strands of pink embroidery floss, work two spider's webs 2cm (3/4 in) up from the bow and 5mm (1/4 in) apart. Change to the lemon ribbon and work two rounds of the roses, then finish the roses in pale pink ribbon.

4 Work two ribbon stitch buds in pink ribbon, as on the stitch diagram, then using two strands of green embroidery floss, work the leaves in fly stitch, with a straight stitch into the centre of the bud.

5 Using green ribbon, work four ribbon stitch leaves around the spider's web roses.

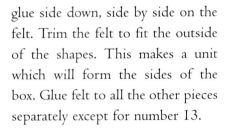

To make up the box

I Using the sharp craft knife, cut out the six templates A to F on page 81 in card or plastic. Use the templates to cut the specified number of pieces from the stiff card and

 Merrilyn bow

 spider's web rose

 fly stitch and straight stitch

 ribbon stitch

number them, as follows:

4 from template A (nos 1, 2, 3, 4)
2 from template B (nos 6 and 7)
2 from template C (nos 5 and 11)
2 from template D (nos 8 and 9)
1 from template E (no. 10)
2 from template F (nos 12 and 13)

Cut out the inner circle from one of the pieces cut from template F (piece number 12).

2 Score the right-hand side of pieces 1 to 4 along the dotted line shown on template A. Spread a thin layer of glue on the unscored side of these pieces, then lay them,

glue side down, side by side on the felt. Trim the felt to fit the outside of the shapes. This makes a unit which will form the sides of the box. Glue felt to all the other pieces separately except for number 13.

3 Place the lemon yellow silk fabric, right side down, on the work surface, then place the sides of the box on top, felt side down, and trim the silk to within 1.5cm (⅝ in) of the sides (see diagram 1 on page 82). Do the same with number 5 (the bottom of the box).

4 Brush a thin line of glue round the edges of the unfelted side for both the sides and the bottom of the box. Working on the unit for the sides of the box first, fold over the two short sides of the silk onto the card and press evenly to stick them down. Fold in the corners, then fold over and stick the two long sides. Repeat for the bottom of the box.

5 Form the unit for the sides of the box into a box shape by bringing the two short sides together, with the lemon silk on the outside. Using sewing thread and

---

the curved needle, ladder stitch the two short sides together (see diagram 2 on page 82). Place the bottom of the box in position, again with the lemon silk on the outside and stitch in place. This makes the base of the box.

6 Numbers 6 to 10 are the inside and base lining pieces, number 11 is the lid lining. Glue pieces of cream lining silk to each of these separately in the same way as for piece number 5.

7 Brush a thin layer of glue over the unfelted side of pieces 6 and 7, then position opposite each other on the inside of the box. Glue pieces 8 and 9 in the same way and press inside the box on the two remaining sides. Glue piece 10 and press into the base of the box.

8 Lay piece number 12 on the wrong side of the lemon yellow fabric, felt side down, and cut round the silk allowing 4cm (1½ in) extra all round each side of the card.

9 Hold the card and silk firmly in one hand, then pierce the middle of the circular hole with a

pair of sharp embroidery scissors. Cut carefully out almost to the edges of the circle. Repeat all round the circle, working out in segments (see diagram 3 on page 82). Glue round the outside of the circle, fold back the segments of fabric and stick firmly down.

10 Glue lightly round the edge of the circle. Place the embroidered piece of cream silk, right side up, on a work surface and very carefully position piece 12 over it, so that the embroidery shows centrally in the circular opening. Press in place pulling the edges gently to ensure the embroidered fabric is taut, then turn over. Trim the excess cream silk, then lay the small piece of wadding centrally over the embroidery.

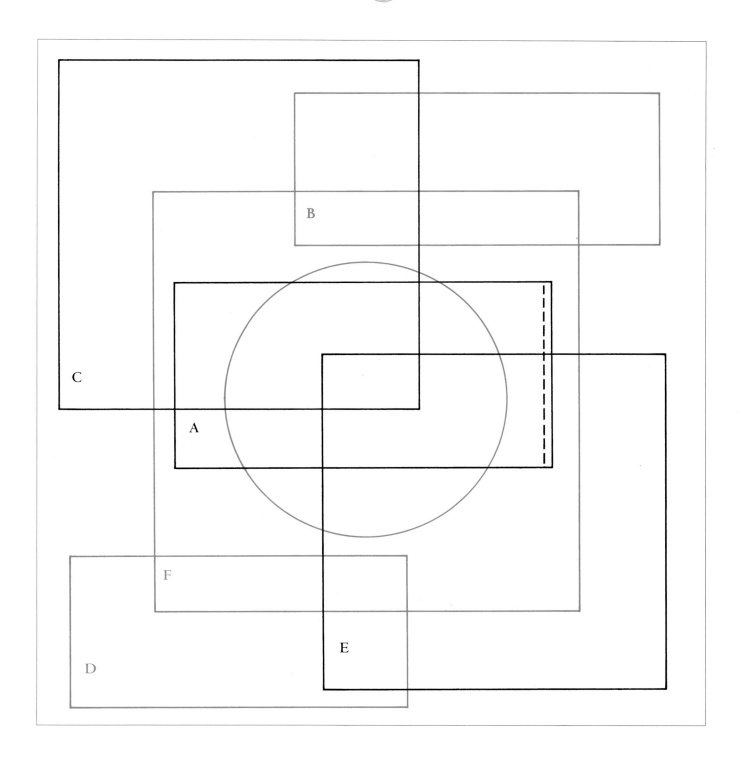

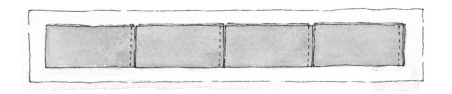

diagram 1

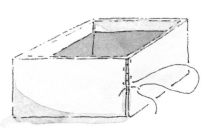

diagram 2

diagram 3

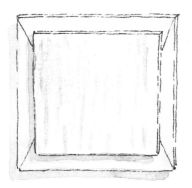

diagram 4

piece 11 and press down centrally on the underside of the lid (see diagram 4).

13 Spread glue very lightly on the pearl beading and position round the outside of the circle on the top of the lid to finish.

NOTES AND TIPS

If you are going to make more than one box (there are two different designs in this book), it is worth cutting the templates from plastic, so that they can be used more than once.

Handle the silk carefully once you have cut round the edge of the inner circle as it frays very easily.

11 Place piece number 13 on top. Glue a 4cm (1½in) strip round the sides of the back of the lid. Fold back and stick down the silk turnings, working on two opposite sides first, neatening the corners, then folding back the two remaining sides.

12 Spread a thin layer of glue on the uncovered side of

PADDED PICTURE FRAME

This picture frame can be used as a gift for many different occasions. For a wedding or Christening photograph, it is a nice touch to make it out of the same fabric as the dress worn by the bride or baby for the actual occasion. I used silk dupion which is an inexpensive but luxurious fabric with a lovely surface texture. The outside measurement of the frame is 30 x 25cm (12 x 10in) and the aperture 16 x 13cm (6½ x 5in) but you could adjust the size to fit your own requirements.

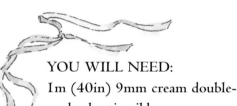

YOU WILL NEED:
1m (40in) 9mm cream double-edged satin ribbon
1m (40in) 9mm medium pink double-edged satin ribbon
1m (40in) 9mm dark pink double-edged satin ribbon
40cm (16in) silk fabric, 115cm (45in) wide
embroidery hoop or frame
no. 18 chenille needle
crewel needle or similar
tailor's chalk or dressmaker's marking pencil
50cm (20in) 4mm off-white silk ribbon
pink sewing thread to tone with satin ribbons
a length of light lemon embroidery floss

a length of light pink embroidery floss
1m (40in) gold embroidery thread
gold coloured sewing thread
1m (40in) 1.5cm wide wire-edged gold ribbon
bow maker (optional)
2 pieces of stiff card, 30 x 25cm (12 x 10in) each
1 piece of lightweight wadding, 30 x 25cm (12 x 10in)
fabric glue
2 small adhesive hooks and hanging cord (optional)
1 piece of stiff card, 6 x 25cm (2½ x 10in) for a stand (optional)

To stitch the design

1 Make three cream, two medium pink and three dark pink double-edged satin roses with the satin ribbons.

2 Cut a piece of fabric 35 x 40cm (14 x 16in) for the front of the frame. Mark the centre top of the fabric. Stretch in an embroidery hoop or frame. Stitch the roses onto the fabric, as shown in the stitch diagram on page 84.

3 Using the off-white silk ribbon, work eleven French knots in the positions shown.

4 Using two strands of the light lemon embroidery floss, stitch clusters of three French knots in the positions shown.

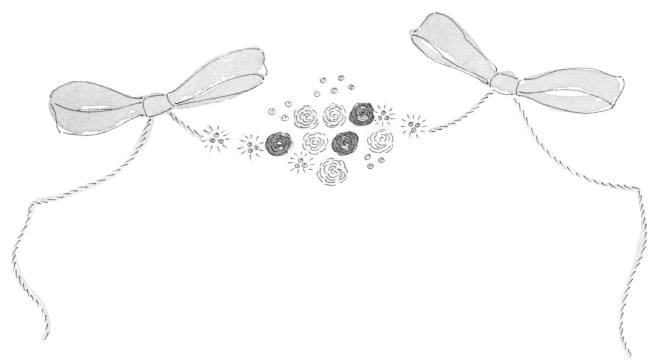

5 Using two strands of the light pink embroidery floss, work straight stitches radiating out from the lemon French knots.

6 Using all six strands of the gold thread and working in stem stitch, stitch the rope on either side of the flowers in the shape shown (it's a good idea to draw it on first with chalk or pencil).

7 Make two small bows without tails in the gold wire-edged ribbon. (You could use someone else's

fingers to get the size right but if you have a bow maker that would be ideal.) Stitch down the ribbon ends using the sewing thread, then stitch onto the silk as shown.

To make up the frame

I Cut a rectangle 16 x 13cm (6 ½ x 5in) from the middle of one of the pieces of card, leaving a 7cm (2¾in) border at top and bottom and 6cm (2½in) at the sides. Cover the front of the frame with wadding and glue down.

double-edged satin rose

French knot

straight stitch

stem stitch

84

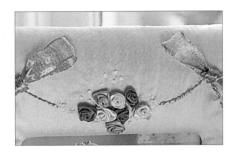

2 Spread a little glue over the wadding. Lay the embroidered fabric centrally over the frame front, right side up, and gently press in position.

3 Pierce the middle of the fabric covering the aperture with a pair of sharp embroidery scissors and cut diagonally out to each corner of the frame to within 5mm (¼ in) of the corner. Put a small spot of glue at each corner to prevent fraying. Trim off the points. Glue the edges of the sides of the aperture at the back and fold the fabric back onto it.

4 Fold the fabric round the outer edges of the frame front to the back and glue down. Make small cuts around the edges to allow the fabric to stick to the back of the card without puckering and mitre the corners carefully.

5 Cut a second piece of fabric 30 x 35cm (12 x 14in) to cover the front of the second piece of card (the back board), glue and stick, turning the excess to the back.

6 Cut a third piece to the same dimensions, turn under a 2.5cm (1in) hem and machine stitch all round. Glue this piece to the reverse of the back board.

7 Place the two boards wrong sides together and, using a curved needle, ladder stitch the top and two sides together, leaving the bottom open to insert a photo.

8 If you wish to hang your frame on the wall you can buy small self adhesive hooks but if you wish it to stand, then you need to cut a third piece of card in the shape shown (see diagram). Score along the dotted line to make a hinge. Cover it in fabric which should be cut 1.5cm (½in) bigger than the card to wrap round the edges. Cut another piece of fabric to cover the back of the stand below the hinge and glue in place. Glue the area above the hinge very firmly to the centre back of the frame, so that the

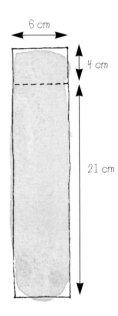

6 cm

4 cm

21 cm

bottom is level with the bottom of the frame.

NOTES AND TIPS

If you are working with silk or any fabric which tends to fray easily, you can stick a length of pearl beading around the inside edge in order to hide any of the little cuts that may show on the front of the work. (They do tend to run when you are pulling the fabric firm over the cardboard frame.)

CHRISTENING GOWN

I have worked ribbon embroidery onto a number of Christening gowns. It looks fabulous. I usually work in the same colour as the fabric (white or cream) but for the photograph, so that you are able to see my design better, I have used ice cream coloured ribbons. I have made up this little dress in silk dupion with a lace edging on the skirt and the cuffs and ribbon bows at the sleeves. Any shop-bought or home-made dress is suitable provided it has a plain yoke like the one shown here.

YOU WILL NEED:

I purchased Christening gown
or
silk fabric to make one (amount as pattern instructions)
tailor's chalk or dressmaker's marking pencil
embroidery hoop or frame
no. 18 chenille needle
crewel needle or similar
1.5m (1²/₃ yds) 7mm pale pink silk ribbon
4.5m (4³/₄ yds) 4mm pale lemon silk ribbon
50cm (20in) 7mm pale green silk ribbon
ivory embroidery floss
1 2–3g packet seed pearl beads
beading needle
sewing thread to tone with beads and ribbons

To stitch and make up the design

1 If you are making the dress yourself, lay the pattern pieces on the fabric and either draw or tack round the shapes.

2 Mark the centre of the front yolk. Stretch this area in an embroidery hoop or frame. Do not cut the pattern pieces until all the embroidery is completed to minimise the fraying.

3 Using the pink and the lemon ribbons, work a pre-gathered rose and stitch it in the centre spot of the yoke. Work two more roses and stitch on either side of the centre rose, each 4cm (1½ in) away from it.

4 Using the lemon ribbon, work two five-petal flowers in ribbon stitch, each one centrally in between and below the pre-gathered roses (see stitch diagram on page 88).

5 Using the green ribbon, work three ribbon stitch leaves above the roses positioned as shown in the diagram.

6 Using two strands of the embroidery floss, stitch four lazy daisy flowers in the positions shown.

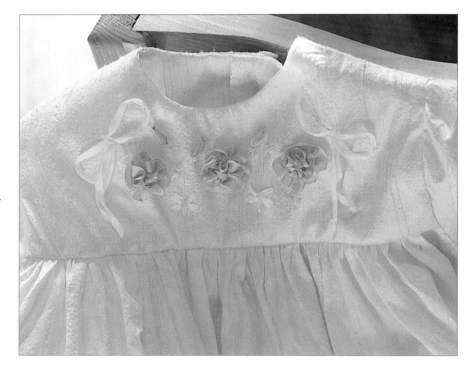

Merrilyn bow
pre-gathered rose
lazy daisy stitch
ribbon stitch
bead

7 Using the pale lemon ribbon, work two Merrilyn bows with long twisted tails on either side of the work already stitched.

8 Sew the seed pearls in the centre of the yellow flowers and at the base of the leaves.

9 On the centre front of the skirt and approximately 15cm (6in) up from the bottom, work three pre-gathered roses in the same colours and spaced as on the yolk. Work the yellow ribbon flowers, the green leaves and the ivory embroidery floss flowers, then sew on the seed pearls as before.

10 Using chalk or pencil, draw two parallel lines as in the template below. Work along the line with the lemon ribbon in ribbon stitch to the end.

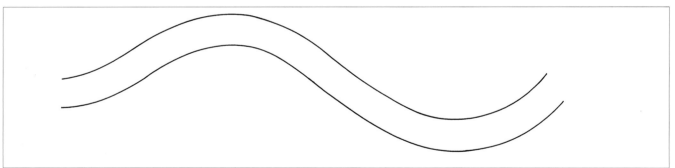

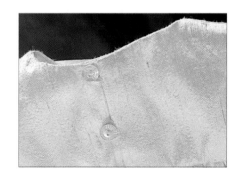

11 Sew a seed pearl at the top of each ribbon stitch.

12 Cut out and make up the dress according to the pattern instructions. I worked a looped button carrier to fit over the pearl buttons as a finishing touch.

FOUR GREETINGS CARDS

Silk ribbon embroidery is a perfect medium for hand-stitched greetings cards. I have given four designs here with specific uses, however, all but the Christmas card could be mixed and matched for other occasions. Before mounting your work, you may like to put a small amount of wadding at the back of the embroidery. This pads the work and makes for a better finish. The Christmas card has a simple little design but it is quite quick and definitely fun to work. Instead of the more usual daffodils for the Mother's Day card, I thought some very simple irises would be good. I used green moiré taffeta as the background fabric but other fabrics, such as linen, cotton chintz or silk dupion would work just as well. The wedding and birthday cards have both been mounted in specially cut cards with stencilled butterflies as an additional decoration. They could both be displayed in purchased mounts with a 7.5cm (3in) square aperture.

YOU WILL NEED:

Christmas card

1 piece of cream silk to fit the
    card mount plus a small overlap
2m (2¼yds) each of three
    different shades of 4mm green
    silk ribbon
8 bright beads in Christmas
    colours
beading needle
sewing thread for beads
scrap of 4mm gold ribbon
1 card mount

Mother's Day card

1 piece of green taffeta to fit the
    card mount plus a small overlap

50cm (20in) 4mm blue/purple
    silk ribbon
crewel needle or similar
matching green embroidery floss
75cm (30in) 4mm green silk
    ribbon
1 card mount

Wedding card

1 piece of cream silk to fit the
    card mount plus a small overlap
75cm (30in) 4mm tan silk
    ribbon
75cm (30in) 7mm orange silk
    ribbon
75cm (30in) 7mm green silk
    ribbon
75cm (30in) 4mm pale green
    silk ribbon

a length of tan embroidery floss
crewel needle or similar
1 card mount
or
1 piece of card, 51 x 15cm
    (20 x 6in)
butterfly stamp (optional)
variegated stamp ink pad
    (optional)
embossing powder (optional)
heat gun (optional)

Birthday card

1 piece of green satin to fit the
    card mount plus a small overlap
50cm (20in) 4mm pale orange
    silk ribbon
scrap of pale 4mm brown silk
    ribbon

25cm (10in) 7mm orange silk
  ribbon
25cm (10in) 7mm dull green
  silk ribbon
a length of yellow embroidery
  floss
crewel needle or similar
1 card mount
or
1 piece of card, 51 x 15cm
  (20 x 6in)
butterfly stamp (optional)
variegated stamp ink pad
  (optional)
embossing powder (optional)
heat gun (optional)

All cards
no. 18 chenille needle
small amount of wadding
  (optional)
13cm (5in) embroidery hoop
tailor's chalk or dressmaker's
  marking pencil
fabric glue

To stitch the Christmas card

1 Make a template from the
  Christmas tree shape on page

97 and draw the outline onto the
centre of the fabric using chalk or
pencil. Stretch the fabric in a hoop.

2 Using one green ribbon at a
time, work French knots scat-
tered randomly over the whole tree
shape. Work from top to bottom
and avoid having too many lengths
of connecting ribbons between
stitches at the back of the work.

3 When the whole area of the
tree has been worked, stitch the
beads at the ends of the branches.

4 Using the gold ribbon, stitch a
triangle of three straight
stitches at the top of the tree. Your
work is now ready to mount as
described below.

NOTES AND TIPS

It is essential that you work the
Christmas tree design in a hoop or
you may get puckering.

To stitch the Mother's Day card

1 Mark the centre of the fabric with tailor's chalk or pencil and stretch it in a hoop.

2 Position the first flower head about 2cm (¾ in) up from the centre point. Work the flower using the blue/purple ribbon. First make a lazy daisy stitch about 1cm (⅜ in) in size. Take the needle to the back of the work and bring it out again below and to the right of the bottom of the lazy daisy stitch. Pass behind the lazy daisy stitch using the eye of the needle first (to avoid catching the ribbon), then go back down into the fabric below and to the left of the lazy daisy.

3 Work a second flower head either to the right or to the left of the first, placing it at a slightly different height to add interest. Work a flower bud by just working one simple straight stitch.

4 Using two strands of the embroidery floss, work the stalks in long straight stitches, taking them 2cm (¾in) below the centre mark.

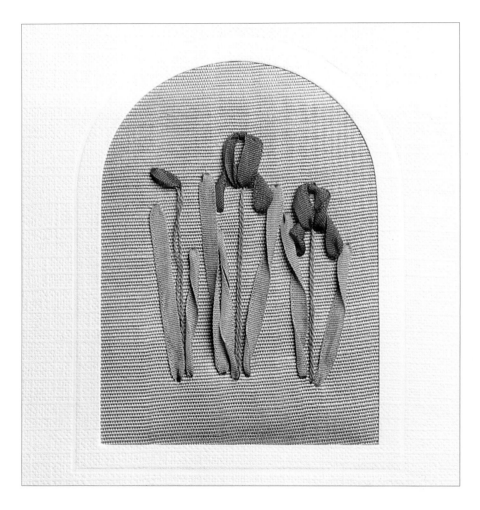

5 Using the green ribbon, work the leaves in long straight stitches, allowing the ribbon to twist to add more dimension to your work.

6 The embroidery is now ready to mount in its card, as described on page 96.

To stitch the wedding card

1 Make a template from the butterfly shape given on page 97 and draw the outline onto the centre of the fabric using tailor's chalk or pencil. Alternatively, draw on your own butterfly shape. Stretch the fabric in a hoop.

2 Using the tan ribbon, work the body of the butterfly in a whipped running stitch.

3 Change to the orange ribbon and work the outer half of the right wing in straight stitches of varying lengths but working to the drawn shape of the outer wing.

4 Change back to the tan ribbon and work again in straight stitches of varying lengths from the body up to the orange stitches.

5 Work the left wing of the butterfly in the same way using the 7mm green ribbon for the outer part and the 4mm pale green ribbon for the inner.

6 Using two strands of embroidery floss, work two pistil stitches for the feelers.

7 The card is now ready to mount. If using a bought mount, follow the instructions below. If cutting your own, trace the leaf template on page 97 onto the left half of the middle section of the card and cut out. Mount the embroidery as described below.

8 To add the cut-out butterflies, work as follows: using the butterfly stamp and ink pad, stamp the card to the right of the embroidery. Repeat in the right-hand corner of the card.

9 Stamp a spare piece of card, then sprinkle with embossing powder. Use a heat gun to produce a raised shine. Repeat.

NOTES AND TIPS
The colours of the ribbon were chosen after the stencilling was completed to match the colours of the stencil ink.

10 Cut out the two butterflies, glue just the body section and stick over the previously stamped butterflies.

To stitch the birthday card

1 Mark the centre of the fabric with tailor's chalk or pencil and stretch it in a hoop.

2 Using the pale orange silk ribbon, work a straight stitch at the centre point, then a series of other straight stitches in the positions shown in the stitch diagram opposite.

3 Next work a five-petal flower in ribbon stitch in the position shown in the diagram.

4 Change to the pale brown ribbon and work a couple of buds using straight stitch as shown.

5 Using the orange ribbon, work two ribbon stitches as shown.

6 Using two strands of the yellow embroidery floss, work a straight stitch up the centre of the two orange petals.

7 Mark a point approximately 2cm (¾in) below the centre. Using two strands of the green embroidery floss, work stalks in straight stitch bringing them down to the point just marked. Join the foliage stems with a large back stitch and work fly stitch with a straight stitch into the petals to form the calyxes.

8 Using the green ribbon, work four ribbon stitch leaves to cover the base of the stalks.

9 Mount the card as described for the wedding card above.

⬯	straight stitch
⬱	ribbon stitch
⩔	fly stitch and straight stitch
∘	bead

To make up all the cards

1 Place the card mount face up and opened out. Slide the embroidery underneath the opening until the design is central. Mark the edges of the card on the fabric. Remove the fabric and trim it back 3mm (⅛ in) beyond the marked lines, so that no fabric can be seen at the edges of the card.

2 Glue the reverse of the card opening and all over the back of the right-hand flap. Place the fabric back in position and make sure it is taut. Place the wadding

trimmed to fit over the opening (if using) and fold over the right-hand flap (see diagram). Press until the glue holds firm but be careful not to flatten the embroidery.

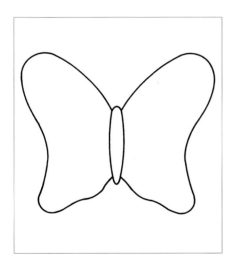

PICTURE BOW

Picture bows draw attention to a favourite photograph or painting as well as adding a nice decorative touch to the furnishings of the room. Choose a colour which will tone in with both the picture and the interior decoration. I have chosen an aqua silk in keeping with the beach scene and thought it would also be interesting to theme the work on the bow tails with the picture it was going to display.

YOU WILL NEED:

1m (1yd) aqua silk dupion, 115cm (45in) wide

tailor's chalk or dressmaker's marking pencil

embroidery hoop

no. 18 chenille needle

crewel needle or similar

1 skein mid-coral embroidery floss

1m (40in) 7mm light coral silk ribbon

50cm (20in) 7mm dark coral silk ribbon

a length of dark coral embroidery floss

aqua sewing thread

1 curtain ring for hanging

To stitch the design

1 Cut two strips, 18cm (7in) wide and to the length required. These make the tails for the bow, so will stretch from the bow above the picture to hang beneath it. Make a template from the shell shape on page 101 and transfer to the end of one of the bow tails, 12cm (4¾in) from the base and 2.5cm (1in) from the left-hand edge, using either tailor's chalk or pencil. Stretch this area in an embroidery hoop.

2 Using two strands of the mid-coral embroidery floss, work in satin stitch to block the area shown in the stitch diagram opposite.

3 Change to the light coral ribbon and work the area shown in straight stitch. Do not allow the ribbon to twist but do work fairly loosely so that the ribbon curls.

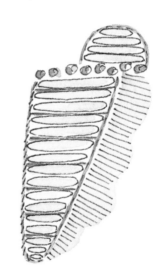

～～	stem stitch
⌒	straight stitch (ribbon)
------	back stitch
⊚	French knot
⦀	satin stitch

4 Using the dark coral ribbon, work the area shown with double wrap loose French knots.

5 Change to the dark coral embroidery floss and work the centre line of the shell in back stitch using two strands only. With the same thread, work long straight stitches across the light coral ribbon. To finish off, still using the dark coral embroidery floss, stitch along the outside edge of the light coral ribbon in stem stitch.

6 Repeat the embroidery on the second bow tail reversing the template and positioning it 2.5cm (1in) from the right-hand edge.

To make up the bow

1 From the remaining silk, cut a piece 19 x 60cm (7½ x 23⅝ in) on the cross. This is for the main part of the bow.

2 Fold lengthways with right sides together. Pin and machine stitch, taking a 1cm (⅜ in) seam allowance. Turn right side out so that the seam is in the middle of one side.

diagram 1

diagram 2

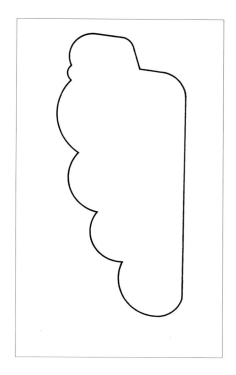

NOTES AND TIPS

If you decide to work your own design, keep it fairly simple, so that it complements the picture on display and is not over-bearing.

3 Fold the ends into the middle to make the bow, pleat and secure by hand (see diagram 1).

4 Cut a small piece of the silk, approximately 6 x 12cm (2½ x 4¾in) and hem all sides. Gather at each short end and fold round the centre of the bow, pulling in the middle slightly. Secure by hand at the back of the bow.

5 Fold the two strips for the bow tails in half lengthways, right sides together, and machine stitch down the long side and the bottom short side, 1cm (⅜in) from the

edge. Form the pointed bottom by stitching a line from the bottom folded edge to 8cm (3⅛in) of the way up the seamed edge (see diagram 2). Trim the excess fabric at the corner.

6 Turn right side out and press. Pleat the top end of the tails, then stitch behind the bow by hand. Finally stitch a curtain ring to the back of the bow for hanging.

FOLK QUILT SAMPLER

I have seen many small patchwork samplers hung on the walls of houses in the States and have always thought they give out a feeling of warmth and friendliness. This has inspired me to create an American folk art style sampler in ribbons on a natural calico background. The motifs are not complicated to stitch and this is very good practice for keeping straight stitches straight.

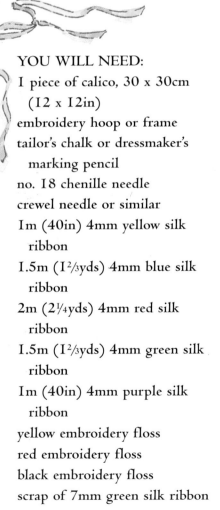

YOU WILL NEED:
I piece of calico, 30 x 30cm
  (12 x 12in)
embroidery hoop or frame
tailor's chalk or dressmaker's
  marking pencil
no. 18 chenille needle
crewel needle or similar
Im (40in) 4mm yellow silk
  ribbon
1.5m (1²⁄₃yds) 4mm blue silk
  ribbon
2m (2¹⁄₄yds) 4mm red silk
  ribbon
1.5m (1²⁄₃yds) 4mm green silk
  ribbon
Im (40in) 4mm purple silk
  ribbon
yellow embroidery floss
red embroidery floss
black embroidery floss
scrap of 7mm green silk ribbon

50cm (20in) 4mm brown silk
  ribbon
75cm (30in) 4mm burnt orange
  silk ribbon
Im (40in) 7mm yellow silk
  ribbon
green embroidery floss
50cm (20in) 13mm green silk
  ribbon
I piece of lightweight wadding,
  26 x 27cm (10¹⁄₄ x 10³⁄₄ in)
I piece of border and backing
  fabric, 40 x 60cm (16 x 24in)
two lengths of 5mm (¹⁄₄in)
  dowel, 33cm (13in) long
Im (Iyd) cord or ribbon for
  hanging

To stitch the design

1 Mark the calico out into a grid of nine blocks, the vertical lines are 6.5cm (2¹⁄₂in) apart and the horizontal lines 7cm (2⁵⁄₈in) apart. Stretch into an embroidery hoop or frame.

2 Using the heart-shaped template on page 106, draw five hearts onto the fabric in the positions shown in the stitch diagram on page 104.

3 Using the chicken template on page 106, draw two chickens onto the fabric. Leave the remaining two squares blank.

4 Work each heart in straight stitch using the colours of 4mm ribbon shown on the stitch diagram and keeping the tension

	straight stitch
	ribbon stitch
	French knot
	stem stitch

6 Using the blue, red and green 4mm ribbons, work the tails in ribbon stitch, worked as described on page 17 but with a single twist in the ribbon. Keep the tension fairly loose to produce a nicely curved stitch.

7 Work the eye using two strands of black embroidery floss in one French knot. Finish the chicken by working the wing in the middle of the body in ribbon stitch using the 7mm green ribbon.

8 For the sunflowers, use brown silk ribbon and work one central French knot followed by two rounds of French knots. Using the burnt orange ribbon, go round once more with French knots.

9 Using the yellow 7mm silk ribbon, work ribbon stitches all around the circle.

10 Using two strands of green embroidery floss, work the stalk in stem stitch.

11 Stitch the leaves using green 13mm ribbon and working in ribbon stitch.

firm and even. Make sure that the stitches are close together, so that they overlap slightly forming a solid block of colour.

5 Stitch the chickens with three strands of yellow embroidery floss in both long and short straight stitches, worked horizontally and vertically, following the shape of the body. Using red ribbon, work the combs and legs in small straight stitches. Stitch the beaks using two strands of red embroidery floss working in straight stitch.

To make the sampler

1 Place the wadding on the wrong side of the calico and pin in place. Machine stitch together along the marked grid lines.

2 Cut two pieces from the border and backing fabric, each 8 x 30cm (3⅛ x 12in). Machine stitch to either side of the sampler, right sides together, along the outer vertical grid line. Open out and press.

3 Cut another piece from the border and backing fabric, 8 x 42cm (3⅛ x 16½in), and machine stitch to the bottom of the sampler, with right sides together along the bottom horizontal grid line. Open out and press (see diagram 1).

4 Cut another piece from the border and backing fabric, 36 x 42cm (14½ x 16½in) and place over the top of the embroidery, with right sides together. Machine stitch along the top horizontal grid line and across the side pieces. Press.

5 Fold back the side panels so that they measure 3.5cm (1⅜in) and pin. Fold back the top and bottom panels so that they measure 5cm (2in) and pin.

6 Turn under the backing piece to fit the front and press. Machine stitch across the top and bottom of the sampler, 3.5cm (1⅜in) away from the top and bottom horizontal grid lines to form 1.5cm (⅝in) channels for the dowel rods (see diagram 2).

7 Slip stitch the back and front of the sampler down the sides, but leaving the top and bottom channels free.

8 Insert the dowel rods into the top and bottom channels and tie a length of cord or ribbon to either end of the top dowel in order to hang the sampler.

diagram 1

diagram 2

ROSE GIFT BOX

Trinket boxes are always a nice present to give and to receive. The construction of this box is the same as the silk box on page 79 but made this time in a pretty cotton fabric appropriate for a birthday or perhaps a Mother's Day offering. The pattern I have worked can be colour matched with any small floral print fabric.

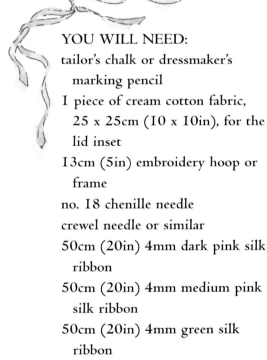

YOU WILL NEED:

tailor's chalk or dressmaker's
  marking pencil
I piece of cream cotton fabric,
  25 x 25cm (10 x 10in), for the
  lid inset
13cm (5in) embroidery hoop or
  frame
no. 18 chenille needle
crewel needle or similar
50cm (20in) 4mm dark pink silk
  ribbon
50cm (20in) 4mm medium pink
  silk ribbon
50cm (20in) 4mm green silk
  ribbon
matching green embroidery floss
stiff paper or template plastic
sharp craft knife
thin card, approximately 3mm
  (1/8 in) thick
I piece of felt, 43 x 26cm
  (17 x 10in)

I piece of floral print cotton
  fabric, 46 x 30cm (18 x 12in)
  for the outside of the box
fabric glue and narrow glue brush
cream sewing thread
curved needle
I piece of plain colour cotton
  fabric, 61 x 30cm
  (24 x 12in), for the box
  lining
I circle of wadding, 8cm
  (3in) in diameter

To stitch and make up the design

1 Draw a 7.5cm (3in) circle in the centre of the inset fabric. Stretch the fabric in an embroidery hoop or frame.

2 Using dark pink ribbon, work the rosebud in two back-to-back side ribbon stitches in the position shown in the stitch diagram on page 108.

3 With the same ribbon, work three lazy daisy stitches in the positions marked. Fill in the centre of these stitches with single straight stitches, to work a blocked lazy daisy.

4 Using the medium pink ribbon, work in fishbone stitch for each rose, working three stitches either side of the blocked lazy daisy.

5 Using the dark pink ribbon, work one or two straight stitches to each rose. Tuck them behind the petals already worked.

6 Using the green ribbon, work ribbon stitch leaves in the positions shown.

7 Using two strands of the embroidery floss and working in stem stitch, work the stalks of the roses as shown.

8 Make up the box following the instructions and using the templates given on pages 78 to 82.

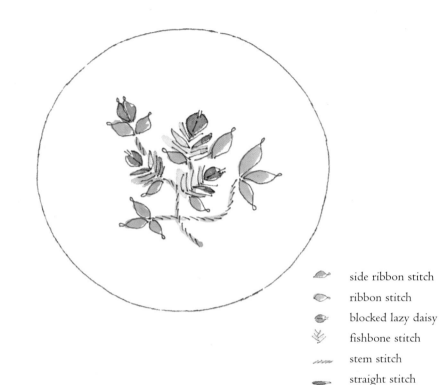

 side ribbon stitch

ribbon stitch

blocked lazy daisy

fishbone stitch

stem stitch

straight stitch

NOTES AND TIPS
I recommend that you use a cotton fabric for box making, it is firm and does not fray too badly.

$\mathscr{S}$PIRAL TOPIARY TREE

Topiary trees over the centuries have always been popular and there is nothing I like better than to see an avenue of beautifully clipped box in a stately home garden. I have created two tree shapes both on a cream damask background and identically framed, so that they can be worked either singly or as a pair. This first spiral tree is a medium level project being largely stitched in French knots. The light and dark sections of the spiral are both worked in two colours to give a realistic shading to the tree.

YOU WILL NEED:
1 piece of cream damask, 40 x 40cm (16 x 16in)
tailor's chalk or dressmaker's marking pencil
embroidery hoop or frame
no. 18 chenille needle
50cm (20in) 4mm brown silk ribbon
6m (6¾yds) 4mm light green silk ribbon
6m (6¾yds) 4mm medium green silk ribbon
2m (2¼yds) 4mm very dark green silk ribbon
1.5m (1⅔yds) 4mm dark green silk ribbon
1.5m (1⅔yds) 7mm gold silk ribbon
50cm (20in) 7mm cream silk ribbon

25cm (10in) 7mm green silk ribbon
a length of green embroidery floss
50cm (20in) 4mm pale blue silk ribbon
a length of yellow embroidery floss
25cm (10in) 4mm green silk ribbon

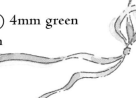

To stitch the design

1 Transfer the template on page 113 to the centre of the fabric. Press the fabric well, then stretch in a hoop or frame.

2 Using the brown ribbon, stitch the sections of the trunk first in a twisted chain stitch.

3 Next take the light green ribbon and, starting at the top of the tree, work French knots within the first section. Dot them about leaving spaces in between. Fill these with French knots worked using the medium green ribbon. The knots do not have to cover the surface completely, it's fine if small areas of fabric show through.

4 With the very dark green ribbon, work in the same way in the second section, filling in with dark green. I have stitched slightly more very dark green knots to achieve an overall darker shade.

5 Continue down the tree in this way, alternating one section worked in the two lighter greens with one in the dark greens. Finish with a section in the lighter greens.

6 To work the basket, first work the gold ribbon in long straight vertical stitches from the top to the bottom of the rectangle, then make horizontal straight stitches with the cream ribbon weaving them under and over the gold ribbon.

7 To neaten the edges, stitch round all four sides of the basket in a whipped running stitch using the gold ribbon.

8 Work the detail at the base of the basket as follows: work loop stitch flowers in the pale blue ribbon with a yellow embroidery floss French knot in the centre. Work pairs of ribbon stitch leaves level with the base using the 7mm green ribbon. Stitch the stalks using two strands of green embroidery floss in straight stitch, then work one or two ribbon stitch leaves using the 4mm green ribbon.

9 Have the embroidery framed by a professional framer. The damask should be stretched onto an acid-free backing board before being mounted in the frame. I have chosen a box frame for this and the following project.

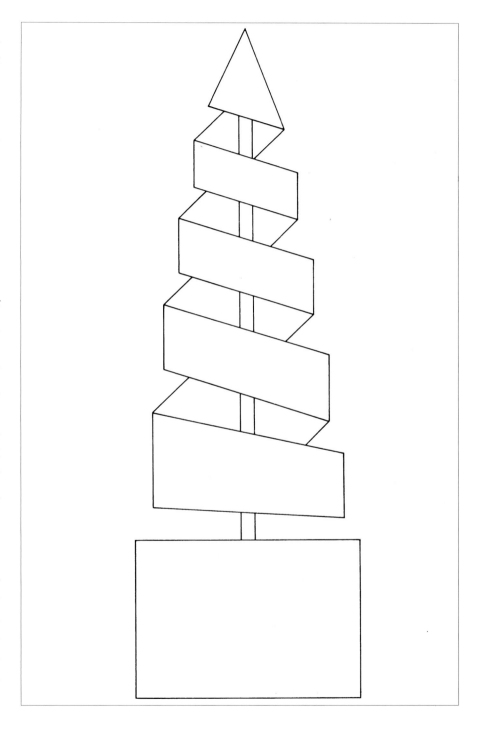

ROUND TOPIARY TREE

This design uses a variety of stitches worked all over the surface to produce an alternative topiary design as a twin to the previous project. This is a more advanced design for the practised silk ribbon embroiderer. It can be adapted to any colour scheme and would also look good on a cushion front.

YOU WILL NEED:
1 piece of cream damask, 40 x 40cm (16 x 16in)

embroidery hoop or frame

tailor's chalk or dressmaker's marking pencil

no. 18 chenille needle

crewel needle or similar

1m (40in) 4mm off-white silk ribbon

1.5m (1²/₃yds) 4mm red silk ribbon

a length of mauve embroidery floss

50cm (20in) 4mm mauve silk ribbon

mustard embroidery floss

1m (40in) 4mm purple silk ribbon

50cm (20in) 4mm yellow silk ribbon

1.5m (1²/₃yds) 4mm blue silk ribbon

gold embroidery floss

2m (2¹/₄yds) 7mm gold silk ribbon

green embroidery floss to match the leaves

1.5m (1²/₃yds) 4mm moss green silk ribbon

50cm (20in) 7mm green silk ribbon

1m (40in) 4mm medium green silk ribbon

50cm (20in) 4mm brown silk ribbon

50cm (20in) 7mm cream silk ribbon

To stitch the design

1 Press the fabric well. Mark the centre of the fabric with two crossed pins, then draw a 7.5cm (3in) diameter circle centrally on the fabric so that its base rests on the centre mark. Remove the pins.

2 Draw a vertical line 5.5cm (2¹/₄in) long from the base of the circle. This marks the position of the trunk. Draw a rectangle at the bottom of the trunk line, 6cm (2³/₄in) wide and 4.5cm (1³/₄in) deep to form the basket. Stretch the marked area in an embroidery hoop or frame.

3 Work the design in the circle using the various silk ribbons and two strands of embroidery floss as indicated on the stitch diagram on page 116. Work from largest to smallest flowers then fill in with

⧤⧥⧦	whipped running stitch
⨯⨯⨯⨯	twisted chain stitch
◉	coral stitch
◦	French knot
▽	loop stitch
◉	spider's web rose
⌐◦	pistil stitch
✇	lazy daisy stitch
◖◗	ribbon stitch
↓	fly stitch and straight stitch

lazy daisy and ribbon stitch leaves making sure that the whole area is richly filled.

The flowers are worked as follows:

red flowers: three off-white French knots in the centre, surrounded by red coral stitch.

mauve flowers: spider's web roses;

purple flowers: French knot in mustard embroidery floss in the centre with five ribbon stitch petals in purple;

blue flowers: French knot in yellow ribbon in the centre surrounded by four to six blue French knots;

white flowers: French knot in gold embroidery floss in the centre, surrounded by five loop stitches in off-white with pistil stitch in gold embroidery floss on each loop.

yellow buds: ribbon stitch in gold

ribbon with detail in two strands of green embroidery floss.

4 Work leaves as follows: round the blue flowers in lazy daisy stitch using moss green ribbon; round the mauve flowers in puffed ribbon stitch using 7mm green ribbon and round the purple flowers in ribbon stitch using 4mm medium green ribbon.

5 Stitch the tree trunk in twisted chain stitch using 4mm brown ribbon.

6 Work the basket using the 7mm gold and cream ribbons as described on page 113 (step 6).

7 To neaten the edges, stitch round all four sides of the basket in a whipped running stitch using the gold ribbon.

8 To finish off, add a few flowers and leaves at the top of the basket and a few leaves at the bottom on the ground as shown in the stitch diagram.

9 To frame the design, see the comments on page 113.

FLOWER GARDEN SAMPLER

I have embroidered some of my favourite flowers on this quilted sampler, some of which I grow in my garden and others which I can only dream of growing! This is a more complex project, suitable for an experienced embroiderer. The flowers are each shown and described separately and, needless to say, could be used in all sorts of other ways to embellish other projects. The ribbons for each flower are listed separately.

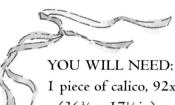

YOU WILL NEED:
1 piece of calico, 92x 4cm (36¾ x 17½in)
tailor's chalk or dressmaker's marking pencil
embroidery hoop or frame
no. 18 chenille needle
crewel needle or similar
1 piece of lightweight wadding, 40 x 40cm (16 x 16in)
3.5m (3¾yds) 3mm dark green satin ribbon
sewing thread to match ribbon and calico
2 lengths of 1cm (⅜ in) dowel, each 48cm (19in) long
60cm (24in) ribbon or cord for hanging

Pansies
50cm (20in) 7mm purple silk ribbon

50cm (20in) 7mm blue silk ribbon
25cm (10in) 2mm yellow silk ribbon
a length of navy blue embroidery floss
a length of green embroidery floss
50cm (20in) 7mm dark green silk ribbon

Lavender
1m (1yd) 2mm lavender silk ribbon
a length of pale green coton perlé
25cm (10in) 2mm light green silk ribbon

Cyclamen
50cm (20in) 7mm white silk ribbon
a length of cerise embroidery floss
a length of yellow embroidery floss

a length of dark green embroidery floss
25cm (10in) 7mm dark green silk ribbon

Forget-me-nots
75cm (30in) 2mm blue silk ribbon
a length of green embroidery floss
a length of yellow embroidery floss
50cm (20in) 7mm green silk ribbon

Primroses/Auriculas
50cm (20in) 4mm dark pink embroidery floss
a length of yellow embroidery floss
a length of green embroidery floss
25cm (10in) 7mm green silk ribbon

Arum lilies
50cm (20in) 13mm white silk
   ribbon
50cm (20in) 7mm green silk
   ribbon
a length of green embroidery
   floss
a length of yellow embroidery
   floss

Chrysanthemums
25cm (10in) 4mm deep red silk
   ribbon
75cm (30in) 4mm tan silk
   ribbon
a length of green embroidery
   floss

Irises
50cm (20in) 4mm blue/purple
   silk ribbon
a length of green embroidery
   floss
50cm (20in) 4mm green silk
   ribbon

Roses
50cm (20in) 4mm light pink silk
   ribbon
50cm (20in) 4mm medium pink
   silk ribbon
50cm (20in) 4mm very light
   green silk ribbon

a length of very light green
   embroidery floss

Daisies
50cm (20in) 4mm yellow silk
   ribbon
a length of yellow embroidery
   floss
a length of light green
   embroidery floss
50cm (20in) 4mm lime green
   silk ribbon

Violets
50cm (20in) 4mm purple silk
   ribbon
a length of yellow embroidery
   floss
a length of green embroidery
   floss
50cm (20in) 7mm green silk
   ribbon

Lilies-of-the-valley
50cm (20in) 4mm white silk
   ribbon
a length of dark green
   embroidery floss
50cm (20in) 7mm dark green
   silk ribbon

Hollyhocks
1.5m (1²⁄₃yds) 4mm claret silk

ribbon
a length of dark green
   embroidery floss
50cm (20in) 7mm dark green
   silk ribbon
a length of light pink embroidery
   floss

Snowdrops
50cm (20in) 4mm white silk
   ribbon
a length of green embroidery
   floss

Red hot pokers
50cm (20in) 4mm yellow silk
   ribbon
1m (40in) 4mm orange silk
   ribbon
a length of green embroidery
   floss
50cm (20in) 4mm green silk
   ribbon

Bluebells
50cm (20in) 4mm pink/purple
   silk ribbon
a length of medium green
   embroidery floss to match
   ribbon
50cm (20in) 4mm medium green
   silk ribbon

To stitch the design

At one end of the fabric, mark out a grid of 16 squares each measuring 8cm (3¼in) square, positioned 10cm (4in) up from the lower short edge and 6cm (2¼in) in from each long side. Stretch the calico in a hoop or frame and work from top to bottom of the sampler, placing the flowers as shown in the key on page 126.

Pansies

1 Starting at the top left-hand square work the group of pansies as follows:

2 Using the purple ribbon, for each flower work two ribbon stitches and one for the bud positioned as shown in the photograph.

3 Change to the blue ribbon and work three ribbon stitches per flower.

4 Using the yellow ribbon, work a small straight stitch into each of the bottom three petals.

5 Using two strands of the navy blue embroidery floss, work three straight stitches onto the yellow stitches and a sizable French knot in the centre of the flower.

6 Stitch the three stalks using two strands of green embroidery floss in straight stitch.

7 Work the leaves using green ribbon in ribbon stitch.

Lavender

1 Using the lavender ribbon, work in small straight stitches in a fern shape as shown in the photograph to form the flower heads. Whip each of the straight stitches, in the same way as for whipped running stitch (see page 24).

2 Using the pale green coton perlé, work the four stalks in straight stitch.

3 Using the green silk ribbon, work the leaves in small straight stitches at either side of the stems.

Cyclamen

1 Using the white ribbon, work the flower heads positioned as shown in the photograph. Each flower has three petals. Work the petals in straight stitch.

2 Using two strands of the cerise embroidery floss, work a straight stitch from the bottom of each petal to about a third of the way up.

3 Using two strands of the yellow embroidery floss, work a single horizontal stitch along the bottom of each flower head.

4 Using two strands of the green embroidery floss, work the stems of the three flowers in stem stitch as shown.

5 The leaves are worked using the green silk ribbon in long ribbon stitch.

Forget-me-nots

1 Using the blue ribbon, work the flower petals in small straight stitches. All the main flowers have five petals but it looks more natural if you work some with just one or two.

2 Using two strands of the green embroidery floss, work the stems in straight stitch, joining three or four flower heads to each main stem.

3 Using two strands of the yellow embroidery floss, work a French knot in the centre of each flower head.

4 Using the green ribbon, work the clusters of leaves in ribbon stitch, remembering to work some of the leaves diagonally across the stems as shown in the photograph above.

Primroses / Auriculas

1 Using the dark pink ribbon, work the flower petals in French knots, varying the amount of knots in each cluster.

2 Using two strands of the yellow embroidery floss, work a single wrap French knot in the centre of each flower head.

3 Using two strands of the green embroidery floss, work the stems in stem stitch.

4 Work the leaves with the green ribbon in ribbon stitch clusters.

Arum lilies

1 Using the white ribbon, work the flower heads as a single ribbon stitch.

2 Using the green ribbon, work the leaves in ribbon stitch near to the flower heads.

3 Using two strands of the green embroidery floss, work the stems in long straight stitch.

4 Using one strand of the yellow embroidery floss, work small French knots up the centre of each flower head to about half way up the white stitches.

Chrysanthemums

I Using the deep red ribbon, work three French knots for each flower head.

2 Using the tan ribbon, work two rounds of coral stitch for each.

3 Using two strands of the green embroidery floss, work the stems in stem stitch and the leaves in fly stitch.

Irises

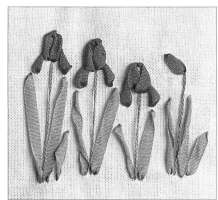

I Using the blue/purple ribbon, work the flowers by first making a lazy daisy stitch, then, bringing the needle up from underneath the fabric, pass the ribbon underneath the lazy daisy stitch and back down into the fabric at the other side (see Stitch Library, page 19).

2 Using two strands of the green embroidery floss, work the flower stems in long straight stitch.

3 Using the green ribbon, work the leaves in long twisted straight stitch.

Roses

I Using fishbone stitch, work the rose flowers with the light and medium pink ribbon. Use the medium pink for the centre stitch then, two light pink stitches, followed by two medium pink. The flower bud just has two back-to-back ribbon stitches in medium pink as shown in the photograph.

2 Using the green ribbon, work the leaves all round the flowers in ribbon stitch.

3 Using two strands of the green embroidery floss, work the stems in stem stitch.

4 Sew the odd leaf or two across the stem in small ribbon stitches as in the photograph.

Daisies

Violets

Lilies-of-the-valley

I Using the yellow ribbon, work the flower petals in ribbon stitch in a circle of seven petals.

2 Using two strands of the yellow embroidery floss, work two or three double wrap French knots in the centre of each flower head.

3 Using two strands of the green embroidery floss, work the stems in stem stitch.

4 Using the green ribbon, work the leaves across the stem in short straight stitches.

I Using the purple ribbon, work five petals for each flower head in ribbon stitch, leaving a definite gap between the top two petals and the bottom three petals.

2 Using two strands of the yellow embroidery floss, work one double wrap French knot in the centre of each flower.

3 Using two strands of the green embroidery floss, work the stems in long straight stitches.

4 Using the green ribbon, work the leaves in ribbon stitch. Make the leaves quite puffy.

I Using the white ribbon, work the flowers in curved rows of about four French knots.

2 Using two strands of the green embroidery floss, work the stems in stem stitch and straight stitch.

3 Using the green ribbon, work the leaves in long ribbon stitch.

4 Using just one strand of the green embroidery floss, work a small running stitch up the centre of each leaf.

Hollyhocks

1 Using the claret ribbon, work four loose double wrap French knots for the bottom of each flower. Work up the flower, increasing the tension of the knots and after two or three rows work in single wrap knots (follow the photograph for the shape of the flower). When you reach the top just work two or three small straight stitches.

2 Using two strands of the green embroidery floss, work one or two single lazy daisy stitches at the top of the flower for buds.

3 Using the green ribbon, work the leaves in puffed ribbon stitch at the base of each flower pointing downwards and one or two up the sides of the flowers.

4 With two strands of the pink embroidery floss, work French knots on top of the ribbon French knots here and there.

Snowdrops

1 Using the white ribbon, work three small straight stitches for each flower head, making the flowers hang downwards. Work a couple of buds with just one stitch, as shown in the photograph.

2 Using two strands of the green embroidery floss, work the stems in stem stitch, then work the leaves in medium length straight stitches.

Red hot pokers

1 Using the yellow ribbon, work three straight stitches which will form the bottom of each of the flowers, then work a French knot at the end of each of these straight stitches.

2 Using the orange ribbon, work the rest of the flower petals in the same way to form a longish rectangular shape as shown in the photograph.

3 Using two strands of the green embroidery floss, work the stems in stem stitch.

4 Using the green ribbon, work the leaves in long twisted straight stitch. The left-hand flower has three leaves, the right, two.

Bluebells

I Using the pink/purple ribbon, work sets of three ribbon stitches for the flower head, only pulling the ribbon through until you get a rolled edge.

2 Using two strands of the green embroidery floss, work the stems in stem stitch.

3 Using the green ribbon, work the leaves (two either side of the flower head in straight stitch and one at the bottom of the stem in ribbon stitch).

To make up the sampler

I Place the square of wadding behind the embroidered calico.

Tack the two layers together thoroughly to avoid puckering when you are machine stitching.

2 Stitch lengths of dark green satin ribbon along the grid lines on the front of the calico using a machine zig-zag stitch and tucking the raw ends underneath. Remove the tacking threads.

3 Fold back the sides and top and bottom of the calico around the embroidery, so that

there is a plain border of 5.5cm (2¼in) at top and bottom and 4cm (1½in) at each side. Fold under the raw edges of the calico at the back of the embroidery, so that they are just out of sight from the front. Pin, then machine stitch across the top edge 2cm (¾in) from the top to make a channel for the dowel. Do the same at the bottom.

4 Hem the back to the front, leaving the channel sides open. Remove the pins. Insert the dowel

pansies	lavender	cyclamen	forget-me-nots
primroses/ auriculas	arum lilies	chrysan-themums	irises
roses	daisies	violets	lilies-of-the-valley
hollyhocks	snowdrops	red hot pokers	bluebells

INDEX

arum lilies 122
auriculas 122
back stitch in embroidery
    floss 26
back-to-back ribbon stitch 18
barrel cushion 34
beads 11
birthday card 96
blocked lazy daisy stitch 19
bluebells 126
bullion rose 21
bullion stitch 21
calico 11
calico hat 61
chain stitch 19
chenille needle 10
Chinese linen blouse 67
Christening gown 87
Christmas card 92
chrysanthemums 123
coral stitch 23
coton perlé 11
couched straight stitch 17
couched straight stitch 17
crewel needle 10
cushions
    barrel 34
    heart-shaped bed pillow 40
    lacy bed 37
    laurel wreath 30
    Thai silk 44
cyclamen 120
daisies 124
double-edged satin ribbons 11
double-edged satin rose 27
dressmaker's marking pencil 10
embroidery floss 11
embroidery frame 10
embroidery hoop 10
evening waistcoat 73
evening wrap 70
fabrics 11
finishing off 13
fishbone stitch 24

flower garden sampler 118
fly stitch in embroidery
    floss 25
folk quilt sampler 102
forget-me-nots 122
four greetings cards 91
frame 10
French knot 21
gift box 77
gold thread 11
greetings cards 91
heart-shaped bed pillow 40
hollyhocks 125
hoop 10
irises 123
lacy bed cushion 37
laundering 12
laurel wreath cushion 30
lavender 120
lazy daisy stitch 19
lilies-of-the-valley 124
loop stitch 22
making a tassel 13
man-made ribbons 11
Merrilyn bow 20
mother's day card 94
napkins 58
needles 10
    chenille 10
    crewel 10
padded picture frame 83
pansies 120
pelmet 53
picture bow 98
picture frame 83
pillow case 50
pinning ribbon 13
pins 10
pistil stitch 22
plastic clip frame 10
pre-gathered rose 25
primroses 122
quantities 11
red hot pokers 125

ribbon stitch 17
ribbons 10
    double-edged satin 11
    man-made 11
    pure silk 10
    variegated 11
    wire-edged 11
rose gift box 107
roses 123
round topiary tree 114
samplers
    folk quilt 102
    flower garden 118
satin ribbons 11
satin stitch in embroidery
    floss 27
sheet 50
side ribbon stitch 18
silk ribbons 10
snowdrops 125
spider's web rose 23
spiral topiary tree 110
starting off 12
stem stitch in embroidery
    floss 26
stitch diagrams 12
stitches
    back 26
    back-to-back ribbon 18
    bullion 21
    blocked lazy daisy 19
    chain 19
    coral 23
    couched straight 17
    fishbone 24
    fly 25
    French knot 21
    lazy daisy 19
    loop 22
    Merrilyn bow 20
    pistil 22
    pre-gathered rose 25
    ribbon 17
    satin 27

side ribbon 18
spider's web rose 23
stem 26
straight 16
twisted chain 20
whipped running 24
stitching beads 13
straight stitch 16
sunflower hat band 64
tablecloth 58
tailor's chalk 10
tapestry frame 10
tassels 13
templates 12
    Christening gown 90
    Christmas card 97
    folk quilt 106
    gift box 81
    heart-shaped bed pillow 43
    leaf 97
    pelmet 54
    picture bow 101
    spiral topiary tree 113
    Thai silk cushion 49
    tieback 54
    wedding card 97
tension 13
Thai silk cushion 44
threads 11
    coton perlé 11
    embroidery floss 11
    gold 11
tiebacks 53
topiary trees 110, 114
twisted chain stitch 20
variegated ribbons 11
violets 124
washing 12
wedding card 94
whipped running stitch 24
wire-edged ribbons 11

ACKNOWLEDGEMENTS

The enjoyment I have had from writing this book has been immeasurable. I have made a number of new friends and acquaintances, and I apologise if I fail to mention their names but I do appreciate everything they have done for me.

There are various people who have been of great help and encouraged me. It is difficult to know in which order they should be thanked but first and foremost must be Rosemary Wilkinson, who asked me to write this book, then throughout has shown me great patience and gentle encouragement. Secondly must be Jane Lang, a dear friend and extremely competent needlewoman. Jane had, from my sometimes very vague descriptions, to turn all my embroidery into actual finished items. Despite having a young family, she always managed to finish projects within very tight deadlines. Thank you Jane, I am indebted. Many thanks to Pat Garfield and Audrey Willows, two past students. Audrey produced the two gift boxes and Pat designed and worked the butterfly cards, both are very competent ribbon embroiderers.

To Enid Garner, who made the Evening Waistcoat, thank you.

To my friend Helen, who helped me out on many occasions, taking my tribe of children despite the fact she has a tribe of her own.

Lastly, to my family. My children, who were very enthusiastic about my work, and, despite the fact that I had to work solidly through the summer holiday, never once complained about the lack of outings. My husband, Richard, to whom I am devoted, thank you for believing in me even though I had doubts.

SUPPLIERS

The Author and Publishers would like to thank Mokuba ribbons and Offray ribbons for supplying their products for use in the projects.
If you experience difficulty in obtaining the materials you require from your local craft and department stores, the following addresses will be of help:

United Kingdom
Audrey Willows &
Pat Garfield
43, Elmore Road
Netherton
Peterborough
Cambs
(Pat and Audrey will make up boxes with your own fabric choice.)
Tel: (01733) 269893

Boo!
1st Floor
25 Silver Arcade
Silver Street
Leicester
(Supplier of calico hat)
Tel: (0116) 262 0401

Creativity Needlecrafts
45-47 New Oxford Street
London WC1
(Specialist supplier of needlecrafts - mail order)
Tel: (0171) 240 2945

Fred Aldous Ltd
PO Box 135
37 Lever Street
Manchester 1
M60 1UX
(Suppliers of craft materials-mail order)
Tel: (0161) 236 2477
Fax: (0161) 236 6075

Heritage Stitchcraft
Redbrook Lane
Brereton
Rugeley
Staffordshire WS 15 1QU
(Suppliers of YLI ribbons - mail order)

John Lewis Partnership
278-306 Oxford Street
London W1A 6AH
(General)
Tel: (0171) 629 7711

Liberty plc
Regent Street
London W1R 6AH
(General)
Tel: (0171) 734 1234

M. Gastman & Son Ltd
120 Portland Street
London W1
(Suppliers of ribbon - wholesale)
Tel: (0171) 580 0735

Offray Ltd
Ashbury
Rosscrea
County Tipperary
Eire
(Specialist ribbon manufacturer/supplier)
Tel: (0171) 631 3548

Sheena Cable
Silkplicity
The Limes
Peterborough Road
Castor
Cambridgeshire PE5 7AX
(Supplier of Mokuba ribbons and brass findings - mail order)

Specialist Crafts Ltd
PO Box 247
Leicester LE1 9QS
(Mail order)
Tel: (0116) 251 0405

W. Williams & Son Ltd
Regent House
1 Thane Villas
London N7
(Suppliers of ribbon - wholesale)
Tel: (0171) 263 7311

VV Rouleaux
10 Symons Street
London SW3 2TJ
(Specialist ribbon suppliers)
Tel: (0171) 371 5929

Australia
Lincraft
For branches contact:
Head Office
103 Stanley Street
West Melbourne
Victoria 3003
Tel: (03) 762 1751

Lincraft
Gallery Level, Imperial Arcade
Pitt Street
Sydney NSW 2000
Tel: (02) 221 5111

Lincraft
St Martin's Arcade
Hya Street Mall
Perth
Western Australia 6000
Tel: (09) 325 1211

New Zealand
Foote Brothers Ltd
43 Normanby Road
Mt Eden, Auckland
(Ribbon specialists/haberdashery)
Tel: (09) 623 4483

Jonora Needlecraft
Heard Park Shops
170 Parnell Road
Parnell, Auckland
(Needlecraft retailer)
Tel: (09) 379 7733

Manukau Sewing Centre
Shop 19 Manukau City
Shopping Centre
Manukau City
(Ribbon specialists/haberdashery)
Tel: (09) 262 1757

Sullivans
28 Sir William Avenue
East Tamaki
(Ribbon specialists/haberdashery)
Tel: (09) 274 6872

South Africa
Bernina Sew & Knit
53 Sanlam Plaza
Maitland Street
Bloemfontein 9301
Tel: (051) 47 2851,
47 6555
Fax: (051) 47 2537

Bernina Sew & Knit
Southdale Shopping Centre
Southdale
Johannesburg 2091
Tel: (011) 433 3551

Crafty Supplies
32 Main Road
Claremont 7700
Cape Town
(Also mail order)
Tel: (021) 61 0286
Fax: (021) 61 0308

Handicraft Designs
PO Box 447
Underberg 4590
Natal
(Mail order - complete craft kits as well as a wide range of general supplies)
Tel: (033) 701 1045
Fax: (011) 701 1296

Pied Piper
13 Kemsley Street
Central
Port Elizabeth 6001
Tel/Fax: (041) 52 3090

Umbilo Drapers
684 Umbilo Road
Durban 4001
(Importers from the UK and USA)
Tel: (031) 25 7814

40-754-2